SONNY'S

BLUE BENN

November 26, 1982

Larry Cultera

SONNY'S BLUE BENN

FEEDING THE SOUL OF A VERMONT TOWN

CAITLIN RANDALL & PETER CRABTREE

The Story Project
North Bennington, Vermont

Text by Caitlin Randall
Principal photography and book design by Peter Crabtree
Archival photos courtesy of Mary Lou Monroe and Lisa LaFlamme
Library of Congress Control Number: 2021923618
ISBN 978-0-578-32989-5
Printed and bound in the USA by The Studley Press, Dalton, Massachusetts
First printing March 2022
Published by Scribe, LLC d/b/a The Story Project
980 Park Street, North Bennington, Vermont 05257

Franklin "Sonny" Monroe

1941 – 2019

BLUE BENN DINER

HUNT STREET

BENNINGTON, VERMONT

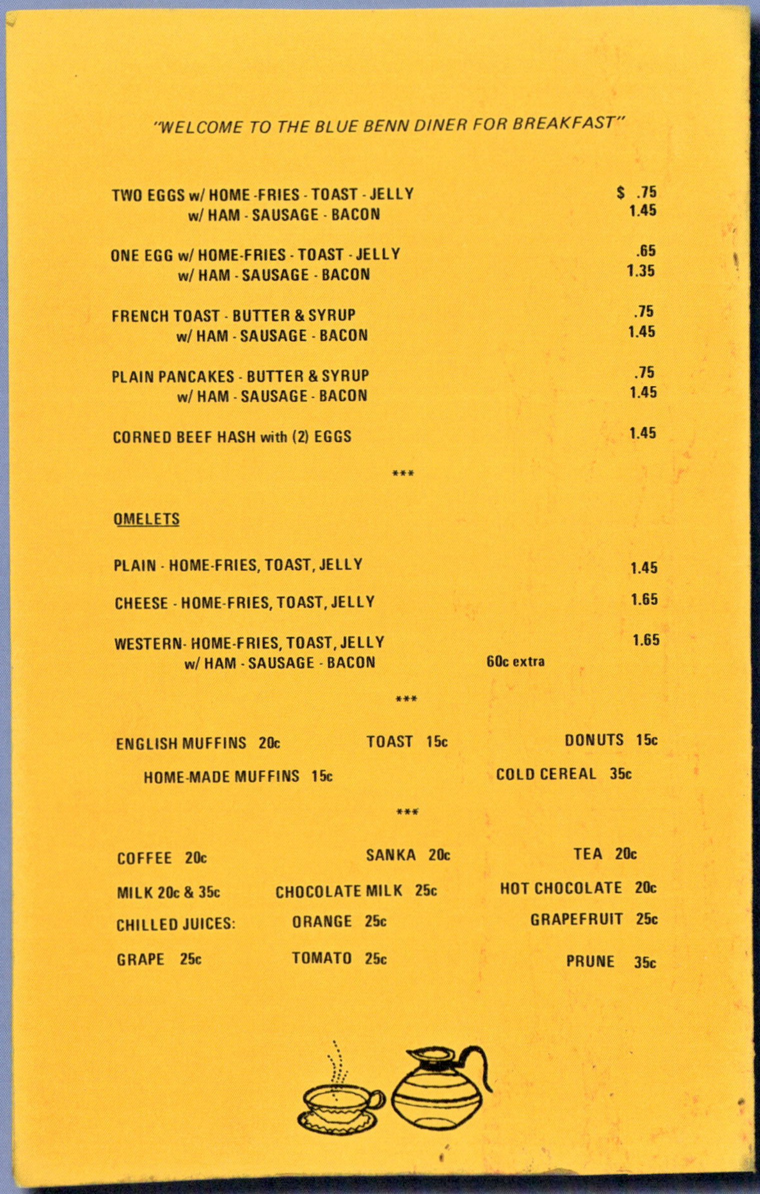

"WELCOME TO THE BLUE BENN DINER FOR BREAKFAST"

TWO EGGS w/ HOME-FRIES - TOAST - JELLY	$ .75
w/ HAM - SAUSAGE - BACON	1.45
ONE EGG w/ HOME-FRIES - TOAST - JELLY	.65
w/ HAM - SAUSAGE - BACON	1.35
FRENCH TOAST - BUTTER & SYRUP	.75
w/ HAM - SAUSAGE - BACON	1.45
PLAIN PANCAKES - BUTTER & SYRUP	.75
w/ HAM - SAUSAGE - BACON	1.45
CORNED BEEF HASH with (2) EGGS	1.45

***

OMELETS

PLAIN - HOME-FRIES, TOAST, JELLY	1.45
CHEESE - HOME-FRIES, TOAST, JELLY	1.65
WESTERN- HOME-FRIES, TOAST, JELLY	1.65
w/ HAM - SAUSAGE - BACON	60c extra

***

ENGLISH MUFFINS 20c — TOAST 15c — DONUTS 15c

HOME-MADE MUFFINS 15c — COLD CEREAL 35c

***

COFFEE 20c — SANKA 20c — TEA 20c

MILK 20c & 35c — CHOCOLATE MILK 25c — HOT CHOCOLATE 20c

CHILLED JUICES: ORANGE 25c — GRAPEFRUIT 25c

GRAPE 25c — TOMATO 25c — PRUNE 35c

Early menu, 1975

MENU

Sonny Monroe in the kitchen, 1977
Rob Woolmington

Mary Lou Monroe, circa 1970s

INTRODUCTION

CHASING THE DREAM

Sonny Monroe was headed home from a 16-hour shift working the grill at the Blue Benn Diner. It was Christmas Eve in 1974, cold and misty. He drove slowly, cocooned in a blast of warm air and the smell of work — cigarettes and fried fat. By the time he pulled the vintage Ford Fairlane into his driveway, Sonny had considered the deal a dozen times, from every angle. Still he worried: would his wife think it was reckless?

Cooking and creating recipes were Sonny's passions. The story goes that when he was three years old, he pushed his chair up to his mother's stove and cracked an egg into a frying pan. "His whole life, he wanted to be a chef, to own his own restaurant. That's all he ever wanted to do," says Mary Lou Monroe, Sonny's wife and business partner for nearly 50 years. "He just was a natural at it."

Determined to chase his dream, Sonny had leased the Blue Benn Diner on that December day; a rundown dive of a place, known to truck drivers, local construction guys and Bennington College students looking for cheap food to get them through all-nighters. The former manager at the diner had bolted on the lease, leaving the Blue Benn available to anyone daring enough to take it on. Sonny couldn't resist the challenge and the chance to run his own restaurant.

When Sonny broke the news to his wife that he'd taken over the lease of a pocket-sized diner, her first reaction was fear. Her second, was uncharacteristic calm. Mary Lou remembers:

I was scared to death, absolutely scared to death. But at the same time I knew it was a good decision, because my heart told me he was going to be a success at this. Sonny was scared, too, but we both knew it was the right thing to do.

I could see where things were going from the time Sonny started working at the Blue Benn. Betty [Manning, the former owner] was totally dependent on him running the place. He was putting in a lot of long hours, because he knew what was coming down the pike. We both knew what was coming, but it wasn't until that night that we dared say it out loud to each other.

We put blood, sweat and tears into that place to bring it around to what it became. From the very start, from that night — Christmas Eve — we were back at the diner, working.

This is a story about a diner and the family that turned a roadside restaurant into a Vermont institution. The tale is told by the best witnesses to the diner's enduring appeal: the regulars who ate there and the staff who made the Blue Benn a legend.

The stories told here also reflect a bigger narrative. They capture a slice of small-town Vermont life and speak to the importance of community hangouts, where people can meet up, linger over a coffee and enjoy the company of their fellow townspeople. All across America, especially in small towns in rural states, we are losing those connections, and with them, a vital thread that helps tie us together.

A good deal has been written about the value of

community gathering spots, with warnings that they are vanishing at a terrible price: loneliness, boredom and a deepening sense of alienation. To thrive, a community requires a place where people can go to be together, to connect with one another. Places, as the sociologist Ray Oldenburg writes, where differences are put aside and people see each other simply as fellow citizens.

Increasingly, [American] citizens are encouraged to find relaxation, entertainment, companionship, even safety entirely within the privacy of homes that have become more a retreat from society than a connection to it.

To have a place available whenever the demons of loneliness or boredom strike or when the pressures or frustrations of the day call for relaxation amid good company is a powerful resource. Where they exist, such places attest to the bonds between people.

Mary Lou

For Cinda Morse, a retired nonprofit administrator and a Bennington resident for more than 40 years, Sonny's Blue Benn Diner was just such a gathering place and so, a critical part of community life in Bennington. Never was that more obvious than in 2020, the year the pandemic forced us all to abandon public life.

The Blue Benn was a place where people just dropped in and where all kinds of wonderful conversations happened that contributed to the collective understanding and getting-along of the community.

Last year [2020] — the pandemic in part, but more the political polarization in America — made us realize how important it is to have places where you can go and sit down next to people and just strike up a conversation. No one checks your party affiliation at the door of the Blue Benn, and you don't make a point of never sitting next to a Republican or a Democrat, you just sit and you get to know each other as people.

It's a lot harder to yell at somebody when you look in their eyes and share a laugh, even if your politics are different.

The Blue Benn's menu, as eclectic as it was delicious, was only part of what seduced the crowds, making the tiny hole-in-the wall one of the most famous eateries in Vermont. The diner itself was a character in its own story.

The Blue Benn is a quintessential model from the heyday of prefab diners. Ordered from the Paterson Vehicle Company, the Benn is a Silk City diner, one of fewer than 500 ever made, every one tagged (the Blue Benn #4815). When it was built, 13 manufacturers were cranking out prefabricated diners, each building a maximum of 250 a year.

The Benn's original owner, Marie York, bought the dining car in her native New Jersey for $17,500 — Silk City diners were proudly the cheapest models available — and in 1948 had it shipped to and assembled in Bennington, Vermont, where it's been a town fixture on U.S. Route 7 North ever since. York, later Mrs. Jolosky after marrying her cook, is said to have named her new diner after its bold blue colors and the Vermont town she'd adopted as home. She ran her roadhouse for just over a decade before moving on in 1960, staying in Vermont but mysteriously never setting foot in the diner again, according to several customers who knew her.

Walk into the Blue Benn today, more than 70 years after it was first uncrated on its near two-acre lot, and little has changed. It's a bit bigger — now measuring 40 by 27 feet compared to 40 by 15 feet. A basement and a kitchen addition have been tacked on to the original building, as well as front foyer with its own azure-blue awning. The diner's original sign in blazing neon script is no longer on display, the victim of a town ordinance demanding it come down. Worn patches pepper the Formica countertop, rubbed down from years of elbows leaning against it, and the tile floor has seen its share of traffic. But the Silk City design, the barreled ceiling, the gleaming stainless steel walls, the blue Naugahyde booths, six in all, and 20 chrome counter stools, still stand proud, still welcoming a steady stream of customers.

One Saturday morning not so long ago, two patrons, both under 10 years old, took a few 360-degree twirls on the Blue Benn's chrome counter stools. They giggled, delighted. Breakfast at the diner can kick start that kind of emotion, even among more jaded grown-ups.

When the Blue Benn is buzzing, it's kinetic. Customers talk to and over each other in a cacophony of conversation. Somewhere in the crowded space, a quarter-operated jukebox — there's a small one at every booth and a couple along the counter — is pumping out "The Lion Sleeps Tonight." The waitresses take orders, fill coffee mugs and haul plates laden with food out from the kitchen. The choreography of their moves is seamless, broken only by a jaunty tease directed at one of the regulars or a shout to the line cook through the kitchen passage. The smell of frying bacon and cinnamon buns fills the air. If there's a lull in the hubbub, it's that the customers have turned to eating — a serious endeavor in the face of the mountain of home-cooked food piled high on the plates.

When Sonny Monroe took over the Blue Benn — he renamed it Sonny's Blue Benn, although he never changed its legal name — diners were marginal operations. Scratching out a living from the diner trade demanded long hours of hard work and a family willing to pitch in to help hold down costs. Under financial pressure, plenty of owners cut portions and hiked prices, but Sonny and Mary Lou Monroe weren't about to follow that course. A native Benningtonian, Sonny knew his market.

Bennington, with its 14,964 residents, is snuggled in the southwestern corner of Vermont and in many ways epitomizes picturesque New England. Site of a Revolutionary War battle, surrounded by the Green Mountains and home to five covered bridges and a prestigious private college, the town attracts its share of out-of-state tourists, "flatlanders," looking for a postcard-perfect Vermont experience.

But behind its frozen-in-time beauty, southern Vermont, and Bennington in particular, has taken some hard economic hits over the years, leaving the town struggling to regain its footing. Factory closures and recession triggered a steady decline in the town and county's population. Indeed, every one of Bennington County's 17 towns had fewer people in 2018 than in 2010. Only very recently has the trend begun to shift.

Bennington's median household income is $44,111, census figures show. That's up from $30,800 in 1998 — not even keeping pace with inflation. The town, the sixth largest in Vermont, is hardly a wealthy enclave that can support a restaurant industry geared to big spenders. Sonny and Mary Lou Monroe understood that.

When Sonny and I took over the diner, Bennington was still a working-class town. I'm going back to when the mills and the Energizer plant were open and when there were plenty of employed construction workers and dairy farmers.

Sonny

"We wanted ... an affordable place for working people."
— Mary Lou Monroe

We wanted to create a business that was an affordable place for working people. A place they could go get a plentiful meal for a fair price.

Lisa LaFlamme, the Monroe's only child, who worked alongside her parents for over 30 years, adds:

It took my mother over 10 years to raise prices at the diner, even when food costs were going through the roof. She knew her customers. She didn't want to lose any of them and she didn't want to offend any of them either — raising prices so they just couldn't eat there anymore.

Sonny's decision to take over the Blue Benn's lease in 1974 was an audacious move. Diners across America were going out of business, hit by a tidal wave of fast-food-chain openings. The couple, still in their early thirties, worked extraordinary hours, sacrificing even family life to turn a scrappy roadhouse joint into a Bennington landmark. They knew they would have to adapt at every turn, like chameleons reflecting the mood of a mercurial public. They tweaked the menu and revamped the diner's look, but most of all Sonny dedicated his time to crafting recipes that would lure locals and out-of-towners alike. His kitchen was his studio, where late at night he created his culinary art, looking for that sweet spot between cost-effective and mouthwatering.

Sonny arrived at the diner most days at two in the morning, ready to do a minimum nine-hour shift. He'd flip on the lights and radio in quick succession. Jazz and big band music blasted into the cramped kitchen. When the place was hopping, Sonny and his then line cook, Brian Carpenter, would churn out 20 to 25 orders at once from two ends of the grill. But late nights were Sonny's alone, giving him the space and time to create his own concoctions. Besides the usual diner food, Sonny cooked up Cajun shrimp quesadillas, spinach and pesto omelets, Syrian roll-ups and the legendary nutburger, a cheddar-walnut patty in a pita pocket with bean sprouts, chopped onions and tzatziki dressing, a notion that took Sonny two years to perfect.

For 13 years before leasing the Blue Benn, Sonny ran the grill at the former Vermont Restaurant, becoming a master of meat dishes. But in his own place, his tastes and menu changed to reflect both a shift in his own eating habits and the evolving tastes of his clientele, particularly

Neon

the student crowd from nearby Bennington College. With little fuss, the Blue Benn kept up with the times.

Willard Boepple, a sculptor and print maker who counts himself among the gang of regulars who frequented the diner every morning, chalks up the Blue Benn's success to the chef's ability to gauge changing culinary trends. As he puts it:

The food obviously had a lot to do with their success. Sonny very smartly took the good parts of the hippie-cooking wave and invented and developed all kinds of great dishes based on those ideas.

And unlike most diners, there was that kind of authenticity about the food, without any pretension. When you ordered turkey, for instance, you could count on it being real, roasted right there, every day.

Sonny proudly plastered the Blue Benn walls with signs plugging his new dishes, printed on pastel-colored cardboard and Scotch-taped to every available inch. It was a bone of contention with his wife, who called the hodgepodge of handwritten signs a sloppy distraction from the elegant stainless steel.

Brian Carpenter, a cook at the diner since 1997 and Sonny's right-hand man, said the signs served an important purpose.

"The signs started when Sonny used to go on vacation," Carpenter once told a reporter. "He'd come back with a new special and couldn't put it on the menu, so he made up a piece of paper and put it up."

While the placards may have caused a marital argument or two, the recipes were a hit. From the 1980s onwards, Sonny's Blue Benn earned coveted citations in *Classic Diners of the Northeast* and *Classic Diners of Vermont* and *Classic Diners of New England*. Stellar reviews rolled in from places such as *The New York Times*, *The Philadelphia Inquirer*, *Martha Stewart Living*, *Yankee Magazine*, *Vermont Life*, *New England Magazine* and the *Roadfood* guidebook.

Despite the accolades, the Monroes never forgot it

Jack Sweet, 1979
Neil Rappaport
Bennington Museum
Bennington, Vt.

Opposite:
Vern Belanger, 1975
Rob Woolmington

was Bennington — the farmers, the lawyers, the nurses and the road crews, their fellow townspeople — who kept the diner in business, every day, every week, every year. Back then, 90 percent of the diner's business was repeat, and 70 percent was local. The Monroes took that to heart.

"... Sometimes in the rush of business life, we fail to say — THANKS — loud enough," a line on their voluminous menu read. "But you can be sure, your patronage is never taken for granted. To serve you is a privilege and a pleasure."

Brenda Eggsware was working the early shift one cool autumn morning, on the kind of day that "leaf peepers" count on in their wanderings through Vermont, gawking at the brilliant red, orange and gold colors splashed across the landscape. But at 6:00 a.m. only a handful of locals stood outside the foyer waiting for her to open up. This was their time, the early-morning gang that met up every day, when they could claim the diner for their own.

As they stumbled in, taking their usual seats at the counter — some even grabbed a booth, unheard of during rush hours — Brenda poured the coffee and called in orders. Most didn't bother explaining what they wanted; the waitress and the line cook already knew. In the lull before the crowds streamed in, the gang would wade into some good-humored gossip. They knew each other's histories and each other's politics and just how far to push their teasing.

Already five hours into an eight-hour shift, Sonny poked his head out from the kitchen to look around at who was there and what they'd ordered. By then, he'd have prepped the day's ingredients, roasted an enormous turkey, baked a batch of blueberry muffins and, with luck, tested a new recipe he'd been considering. The work was relentless and he loved it. But most of all he loved looking out into his diner, proud to know he'd feed a passel of hungry townspeople that day, knowing that great food was only part of the reason they kept coming back. Mary Lou and Sonny had grasped the importance of giving people a place where they could be themselves among themselves, a place a small town in Vermont could call its own. That was their greatest gift to Bennington. That was their legacy to the town they loved.

Vern

Nighthawks
Edward Hopper
The Art Institute of Chicago

CHAPTER ONE

A SHORT HISTORY OF DINERS

Since the very first diners showed up about 150 years ago, they have left an indelible mark on America's cultural landscape. Many of the country's greatest artists, writers and film directors have been drawn to diners, imbuing them with a mythic quality, not unlike legends of the Wild West. It was, after all, chuck wagons, direct ancestors of the modern diner, that fed that uniquely independent hero — the American cowboy.

For writers such as John Updike, Raymond Chandler and Jack Kerouac and film directors Quentin Tarantino and Barry Levinson, diners reflect a vital part of the American spirit. There is a sense, as Michael Stern, coauthor of the *Roadfood* book series, writes, that anything can happen in a diner precisely because they are democratic to the core — anyone can eat there.

The very first diners were horse-drawn lunch wagons that roved the streets of New England's factory districts, feeding late-night shift workers looking for cheap eats. Gaining popularity, the wagons evolved into stationary restaurants known as "dining cars," and later simply "diners."

From their beginnings, they were known for their working-class fare and rough reputations. Diners were seen as unpredictable, dangerous places where shady characters hung out late into the night. New York, Buffalo and Atlantic City went so far as to ban them, worried about their unsavory clientele. Many of the early diners were as scruffy as the patrons who frequented them, cobbled together from abandoned trolley cars, or decrepit boxcars.

By the 1920s, owners began to clean up their act, helped by a New Jersey–based manufacturer named Patrick J. "Pop" Tierney. He started out by building a chain of lunch wagons in his garage and ended up a millionaire, churning out prefabricated dining cars. The factory-built diners may have been generically similar to one another, but their owners were quick to create distinct personalities for their eateries, based mostly on the character of the neighborhood they served.

These refashioned eateries began to develop a more wholesome appeal as a decent place to get a good square meal at a fair price. Their formula was simple: serve homestyle cooking and breakfast around the clock. Keep prices down and quickly adapt to the public's changing culinary cravings.

The diner had become a familiar landmark by the 1940s, not only in factory districts, but also along the fast-growing network of American highways, where truckers became enthusiastic regulars. And when industrial flight from places like Trenton, New Jersey, and Worcester, Massachusetts, decimated the market for workingmen's diners, manufacturers and owners sharpened efforts to attract a new customer base, putting their prefabricated models in unconventional places: seaside resorts, suburban shopping centers, well-heeled neighborhoods and small college towns.

Owners, meanwhile, catered to a new kind of customer — business executives, women clerical workers and college students. As one sales brochure from the late 1940s put it, this was a $12 billion market just waiting for a shrewd operator to play host.

By the 1950s diners were a booming business, appealing to a new generation of consumers in love with sleek design and modern décor. Owners brought in a new more modern look— bold color schemes, Naugahyde booths and chrome counter stools. It was an image that endured, with Hollywood films like *American Graffiti* and *Diner* and television shows like *Happy Days,* helping to reinforce the 1950s diner aesthetic for decades to come. Explains the diner historian Richard Gutman:

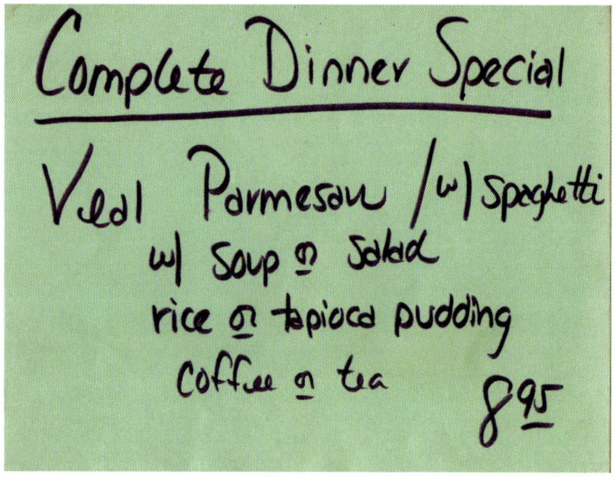

A Sonny dinner special, 2001

Diners changed the aesthetics because the popularity and the success of the business model was outgrowing the old railroad-car imagery and as diners became bigger ... they put on airs. They transformed themselves into something glitzier that made customers feel they should spend more time and more money there.

At the same time, there was more competition. The fast-food business pushed diners into offering more choices, to distinguish themselves and to bring in a wider variety of people.

At their peak, some 6,000 diners dotted the country, from Syracuse to San Diego, with the highest concentration still in the Northeast. "The diner really is a Northeast and Mid-Atlantic phenomenon," Gutman says. "It works best in places like Bennington or Worcester or Allentown — smaller towns ... [where] it takes on its own personality and the personality of the people who are populating it on both sides of the counter."

The historian, who has spent a lifetime researching, lecturing and consulting on diners, estimates that about 2,000 diners are still in operation in America, a whopping 600 of them in New Jersey. The blitz of fast-food chains built in the sixties and seventies whittled away the fortunes of many diners, with thousands going belly up in those two decades. Manufacturers suffered a similar fate, with most out of business by the seventies. To survive in that economic climate required resilience and ingenuity. In Gutman's view, Sonny and Mary Lou Monroe met that challenge. He explains:

One of the things that Sonny Monroe did right was to pretty much hold the price point. He was a cook, and he loved to cook and create recipes, but he also knew his audience. He knew his customers and he knew he couldn't get away with really hiking prices.

And he also knew that people wanted a lot on their plate. So what he did do, I think, was to attract a different clientele precisely by being really inventive about his recipes. Sure, they

Memorable Movie Diners

- Five Easy Pieces
- Pulp Fiction
- Back To The Future
- Groundhog Day
- When Harry Met Sally
- Grease

Opposite: Pennysaver Press, June 1991

served diner food, of course, but he did vegetarian cooking way before anyone else was onto it. …

I think that was brilliant and spot-on. The Blue Benn was known as one of those early places where you could get the "alternative" food you wanted.

***

One of the best-known images of twentieth-century art is a painting by Edward Hopper called *Nighthawks.* The painting depicts an all-night diner where three customers sit silently at the counter, each lost in a world beyond the cherry-wood counter and dull yellow walls. They are alone, even in the company of others.

It's a powerful image and one that's become a touchstone for diner lore. Here, the myth of the diner as a dark and dangerous place has been replaced with an image of it as a lonely haunt. Neither portrayal is true, but as Marie-Pierre Huguet, a Blue Benn regular and academic, remarks, American diners are one of the few public hangouts where sitting by yourself, enjoying solitude and silence, is happily welcomed. That diners can be both boisterous and still is a singular quality that makes them public spaces for all of us —Everyman and Everywoman, together or alone. As she says:

If you wanted to tune out, which I tend to do, you were able to do so. That to me was priceless, because I like to find a silent space, when I'm surrounded by noise. That is one of the strengths of the diner. They allow you to be in the place you want to be or you need to be. So if you wanted to chat, you could. If you wanted to just focus on your food and wait for your bagel to show up, you could. If you wanted silence and isolation, it was there as well. You could always find what you were looking for at the diner.

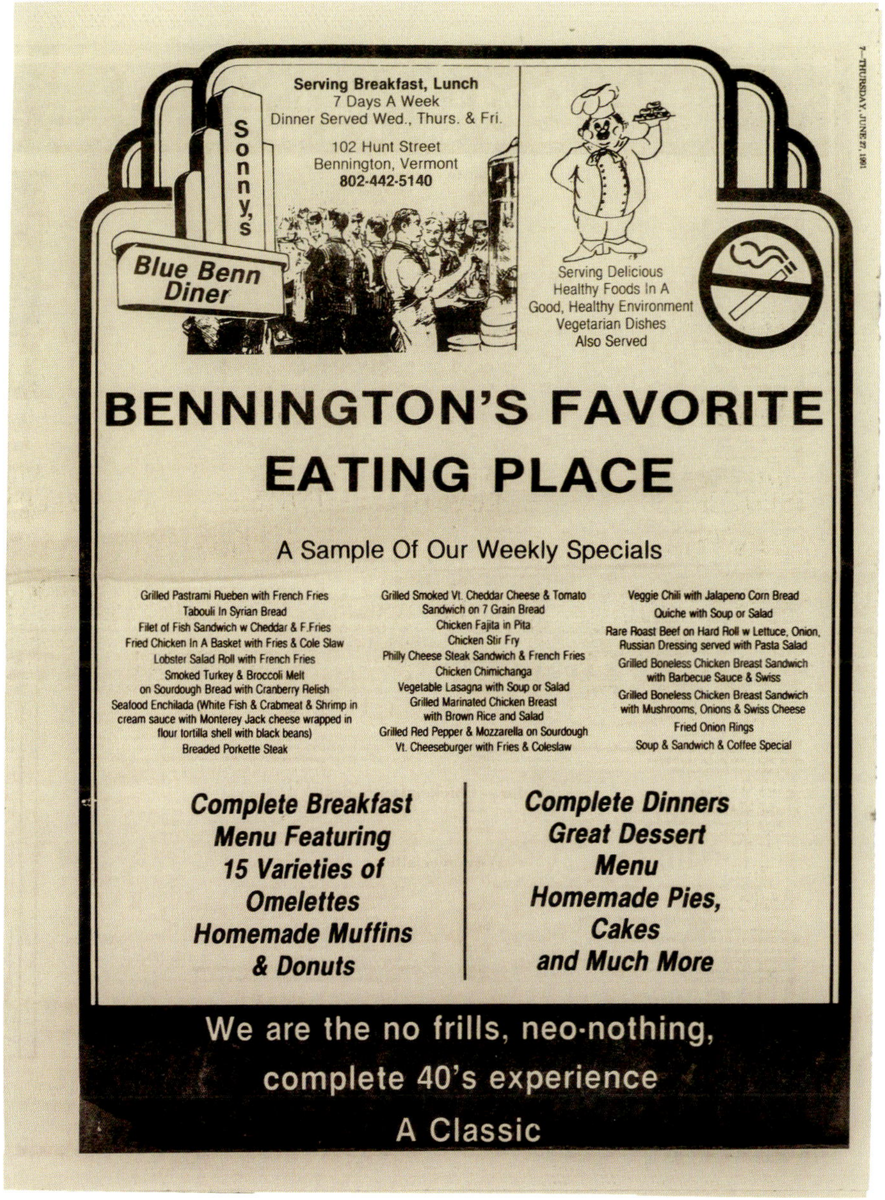

CHAPTER TWO

THE OWNERS: BUILDING A LEGACY

Two cars, a dozen teenagers and just enough cash to cover a couple of Cokes each and the cost of tickets at the roller rink. It was a Wednesday night in 1961 when Franklin "Sonny" Monroe and a group of his buddies pulled into Guptill's, near Albany. The arena was already packed and looking every bit the set of a 1950s teen movie — crowds of bobby-socked roller skaters gliding across the oak floor, girls in poodle skirts and Elvis Presley blaring from the speakers. The Vermont friends rushed to rent their skates, eager to jump into the action.

At 19 years old, Sonny was built like a welterweight boxer, light and strong. He had a handsome face and a reputation as a natty dresser. On that April night, he took his time getting onto the floor. Sonny was not a skater, preferring to people-watch from the sidelines. Earlier, he'd noticed a girl — pretty and shy — and wanted to meet her. Skating haltingly to the rail, Sonny looked out across the rink, hoping to catch her eye. As Mary Lou tells the story:

It was a school night, but my mom let my brother and me go to Guptill's. She drove us there and knew exactly what time it closed and where to pick us up. My parents were tough about curfews.

I saw this guy going around the rink, holding onto the railing, because I don't think he ever skated before. I wasn't really that good either. Our eyes just . . . connected. I don't quite know how it happened, but suddenly we were together, skating.

Not feeling too confident on skates, Sonny quickly invited Mary Lou for a soda. Mary Lou Roy was 17, with wavy auburn hair and dimples. Born in upstate New York, and brought up in a strict Catholic household, she was set to graduate from Shenendehowa High School that June.

We sat down and had a drink, a Coke. And by the next week he was calling me. From that point on, we started sending letters to each other all the time. I have every letter, card, snip of paper that that man ever sent me.

Trust me, the guy was a handsome man. And he really was a classy dresser. I had boyfriends and stuff, but compared to the boys at my high school, he was something else, something special. Luckily, my parents liked Sonny right from the beginning. I was really blessed.

A little over a year later, on September 8, 1962, Sonny and Mary Lou were married. Two years later on August 1, 1964, their daughter Lisa was born.

Sonny's father was a furniture mill worker who crafted detailed reproductions of Colonial pieces. He loved his work, but never expected his eldest child to follow in his footsteps. He knew his son found his creative expression in the kitchen. So it came as no surprise that when Sonny finished North Bennington High School in 1960, he took a job in the venerable Vermont Restaurant where he'd been working part-time through school making pizzas. He stayed there, running the kitchen, honing his cooking skills and

Dance recital, 1968

Previous: First Holy Communion, 1971

learning the restaurant business, until it closed in December 1973. By February, he had taken a full-time job at the Blue Benn Diner. He loved running the kitchen, but was soon convinced he could do a better job managing the restaurant for the owner, Betty Manning. By Sonny's birthday on March 9, the writing was on the diner wall. As Mary Lou explains:

Just from what Sonny was telling me while he was working there, the place wasn't being run well. He worried that the bills weren't being paid. Betty, meantime, was working on Sonny to take over the lease, because she knew of Sonny's reputation from the Vermont Restaurant.

It took until December of 1974 for the Monroes to acquire the Blue Benn lease. "Betty had been grooming Sonny for the job," Mary Lou recalls. "She kept asking if he was interested, but even though I knew it was coming, I was surprised. And that it all happened on Christmas Eve!"

Lisa LaFlamme, the Monroes' only child, tells her own version of the Christmas Eve story, framed from the perspective of a 10-year-old child waiting for Santa Claus.

So Dad comes home on Christmas Eve and says he bought the diner. It really didn't have a good reputation at the time, and the woman that was running it wasn't doing a good job of it. So Dad stepped in and worked a deal out with the owner to take over the lease. My mother was a bookkeeper at the Polygraphic and had no idea about the restaurant business. But there we were, Christmas Eve, and the three of us end up in this grubby diner cleaning. Right from that moment, I hated the place. [laughs]

"I'll always remember Lisa spittin' and sputterin' about that," Mary Lou chuckles.

From that night on, the Monroes devoted their waking hours to the diner, often bumping into family time. As Lisa sees it:

I've always compared the diner to a sibling, someone that I had to compete with, because the diner took a lot of attention. Yes, I had a really wonderful life, and my parents were always there. But the diner was 24/7. *(See interview on page 21.)*

In the first few months, Sonny would leave for work at around two in the morning to start a daily grind of prepping, grilling, roasting — a 40-pound turkey was put in the oven daily — supervising staff and sweating it out in the kitchen where temperatures could reach 105 F.

Mary Lou kept her bookkeeping job, but worked nights at the diner, cleaning layers of grime, scrubbing pots and organizing the accounts.

Sonny was working these ungodly hours. I was working at Polygraphic from the time I got Lisa to school until when she got out around three. … I'd give her a snack, let her change out of her school clothes, get everything ready for the next day and we'd go right to the diner. I would clean and do dishes, and Lisa would sit at the end of the counter, doing her homework. Then, around eight, nine o'clock, we would go home.

By 1977, the couple felt secure enough about the Blue Benn's success that they offered to buy the diner outright for about $50,000, with a loan from First Vermont Bank. Subsequent loans for new equipment or expansion plans were a more casual affair. Mary Lou says laughing: "Our loan officer would walk into the diner, lean over the counter and yell out to Sonny, 'Hey Sonny, how much money you want today?' It was pretty funny."

Blue Benn Diner going smoke-free beginning April 1

MATT KELLY
BANNER STAFF WRITER

BENNINGTON — The anti-smoking forces have taken another beachhead as the Blue Benn Diner bans all smoking starting April 1.

Sonny Monroe, who has owned the diner for 16 years, said he has thought about the smoking ban for three years and finally decided to implement it.

"It was the biggest complaint on the comment cards we passed out," he said. "There were petitions for and against smoking, and they usually came out about even, but the comment cards were very good."

The step will lose him customers, he concedes, but he believes it is the right move. "We're doing this for healthful reasons, not business ones," he said. "We're losing a lot of good friends and customers. But it was a decision I felt I had to make."

"It's hard," he continued. "Some people who have come in here since I've been in business, and they say they won't come back."

While some customers may not return, Monroe hopes others will be drawn by the smoke-free atmosphere to replace them. "I'm hoping it will generate new business," he said. "I had a lot of good remarks along that line, so we may change the clientele. There were a lot who said they wouldn't come in here because of the smoke."

A random survey of customers at the diner on Sunda showed the divisions the issue has created among th customers. "I probably won't be back here again," sai Kathy Smith of Bennington, who was having a after-breakfast cigarette with her coffee.

"We may come here one more time, but that will be it," said Craig Smith, also a smoker.

"Three cheers," said Jan Martin Bopp, of Pownal. "It's long overdue. I affirm and applaud it."

"It would be nice if it were bigger and they could have a section for smoking," said Michael Bushee of Bennington, a smoker who said he would not be coming back.

"I had hoped it was my food that was drawing them and not that it was a place to smoke," Monroe said. "We try to serve healthy food, and to have a negative thing like allowing smoking...."

He thought the hardest hit segment of his business

See SMOKE-FREE Page 18

Matt Kelly

Sonny Monroe sits at the counter of his soon-to-be smokefree diner. After 16 years in operation and thinking about the smoking ban for three years, Monroe finally decided it was time to implement it, even though he admits he will lose some customers.

Monday, March 26, 1990

The Bennington Banner, March 26, 1990

The scramble to make ends meet and win over the locals had eased, but the daily hustle was still nonstop. By then, Mary Lou was working full-time in the dinner. Sonny would leave for work in the middle of the night and at around 4:00 a.m., Mary Lou would wake Lisa out of a sound sleep and half-carry her to the car, where the two would drive to the diner.

We had fixed up a room downstairs in the basement, so that once we got to the diner, we could put her back to bed. She slept in the basement until I would go downstairs and get her ready for school — get her dressed, washed, brush her teeth, and get her to school. It was hard on her and hard on us, but I've never regretted it.

Lisa's memories of those years are mixed. She understands and admires her parents' work ethic and determination, but still harbors sadness:

I had a little bedroom in the basement, just a little bed with a space heater. And my parents would wake me up to go to school. … Usually, my Aunt Pat would take me because she worked at the wood mill in North Bennington and my school was nearby.

Back then you could still smoke in the diner, and we had regular coffee-toast, coffee-donut customers. Every morning they'd be there and the jukebox would be cranking, and you could smell the smoke, and you could smell the bacon, and that's what I went to school smelling like. It wasn't great memories.

If there was ever a time when Mary Lou and Sonny worried that they might lose the admiration of local Benningtonians, it was in 1990, when Sonny banned smoking in his diner. The ban came five years ahead of the Vermont Legislature's move to outlaw smoking in restaurants and hotels, considered a radical move by the state government at the time.

Sonny told the *Bennington Banner* he'd been mulling over the ban for nearly three years and conceded that the move would lose him customers. "We're doing this for healthful reasons, not business ones," he said. "We're losing a lot of good friends and customers. But it was a decision I felt I had to make."

Looking back on the move, Mary Lou argues that it was ahead of its time, health-conscious and, in the end, good business.

We'd practically start taking our clothes off in our cars, because our clothes just reeked, reeked, reeked. We talked about a smoking ban off and on, on and off, many times, and he just said to me, Mary Lou, it's either gonna make us or break us.

We took a poll at the register. We asked the custom-

COUNTER CULTURE'S

1986 diner of the year

SONNY's

blue benn

Counter Culture: A Journal of Diner Appreciation

ers, including the customers that were truly cigarette-coffee-read-the-paper types to give an opinion. … In the end, we lost some customers, really only a handful, less than 10. But how we gained.

Over the years, the diner's fixtures and interior furnishings stayed the same, but Mary Lou and Sonny would expand the diner itself, adding to the kitchen and putting a foyer out front in 1985 — a waiting room for an ever-larger crowd of customers waiting to claim a booth. Kitchen and wait staff were hired as well. By 1990, 16 people worked three shifts, including 12 waitresses, two line cooks and two dishwashers, an impressive hiring spree from the early days when Sonny and Mary Lou ran the place with just two waitresses.

But the crucial change had little to do with the diner's layout or the number of waitresses serving customers. Sonny's Blue Benn got famous. Food critics and newspapers came calling, chronicling "the lure of the Blue Benn Diner that transcends generations and geographical boundaries." They sang Sonny's praises, calling the food "pure bliss" and hailing his willingness to experiment with vegetarian dishes and create inventive fare that kept a wide range of customers coming back for more.

If more evidence was needed, the lines outside the diner were proof of the Benn's enormous popularity. The Blue Benn Diner comfortably sits 44 people, but on any given Saturday — their busiest day — when Sonny was behind the grill, at least half that number would be lined up outside, waiting for a booth or a spot at the counter. Sonny's Blue Benn Diner had become a Vermont legend.

"Sonny was deeply honored. He always wanted the diner, and to see what it became, that was wonderful," Mary Lou says of the accolades. "But in our hearts, we were basically very private people. I just didn't like all the hoopla or whatever you want to call it."

The "hoopla" did, however, give the couple the financial room to travel. And with a staff that rarely moved on — most of the waitresses had worked for the Monroes for nearly 25 years — they were confident the diner was in good hands. They took cruises with friends and Sonny would take a yearly break to Florida, leaving Brian Carpenter, who began working as a cook at the Benn in 1997, in charge of the kitchen. But even on vacation, Sonny would find himself studying menus and judging the merits of far-off restaurants, bringing ideas home to try out in the Benn.

With her parents away, Lisa, who started working in the diner from the time she was in high school, took over the reins as the diner's on-site manager. When her father retired in 2009 and her mother stepped back from full-time duties to care for him in later years, Lisa took over as manager. She took on the role with a mix of pride and resignation:

I was in charge, but I never, ever, ever wanted to be a boss. I wanted to be like one of the other employees. I didn't want anybody to say, 'She's one of the owners.' But, over time, I had to deal with it, because Mom and Dad weren't present anymore. So I did have to sort of step in, but I'm not a boss. I'm not.

For the Monroe family, one favorite of many, many Blue Benn tales, is of the day Bill LaFlamme asked Lisa to marry him. It happened at the counter, in the diner. Of course.

At 19, Lisa was lovely mix of both her parents, inheriting her mother's beautiful smile and her father's soulful eyes. She had graduated from Mount Anthony Union High School in 1982 and began working full-time at the diner. Bill LaFlamme was a few years older and working as a milkman for Fairdale Farms. The Blue Benn was on his route.

"It was so cute," she says, remembering their first encounter. "He brought the dispenser into the front of the diner, so he had to walk by me and we struck up a little bit of a conversation."

That's when Bill's cool act fell apart. Carrying a heavy load and chatting simultaneously, he inched his way backward through the kitchen door, not noticing the laundry basket used for dirty aprons. He stumbled, nearly falling into the basket, before saving himself in a move only a 22-year-old athlete could pull off.

Luckily, Bill's proposal was a good deal smoother.

I was 22 by then and — it's kind of a joke; I guess I gave him a bit of an ultimatum. So it was Saturday and we went to the diner for breakfast. I remember we sat at the counter, at seat one and two. I was eating my omelet, and he romantically handed me the box. No, the ring wasn't IN my omelet like the stories claim. But everyone in the diner started clapping and the place was packed because it was Saturday. It was crazy for a while … the place was rockin'.

Two years later, in 1988, Bill and Lisa were married and five years after that their first son, Matheson, was born, followed by Marcus in 1996. A joy to their grandparents, the boys spent time with both of them, on trips, at their home and in the Blue Benn where Matheson, in particular, learned to cook at his grandfather's side.

Aboard the Starward, Norwegian Cruise Lines

Mary Lou, 2021

Opposite:
Yankee Magazine, 1988
Annie Card

Sitting with Mary Lou in the Monroes' cozy home, it's easy to understand how the Blue Benn earned a reputation for its relaxed, warm atmosphere. Mary Lou delights in making guests feel at home. So much so that keeping her seated for an interview can be a challenge. There's always something to offer, or something to bring to the neatly organized living room; a fresh cup of coffee, a glass of sparkling water, tangy lemon cookies. I wondered if she missed the old days waiting tables.

"You have to be very dedicated and very focused to make the business a success. We gave our lives to it," Mary Lou says, leaning back in a comfy, overstuffed armchair. "When I owned the diner, the phone would ring 10, 12 times a day. That phone never rings now and I'm fine with that. I feel blessed."

On her shoulder Mary Lou wears a pin: a tiny gold angel, wings outspread, looking to be flying. It's a talisman that has taken her through some of life's most difficult moments.

When my mom died she was brought back home from North Carolina to be buried. My stepdad asked if I could find her rosary beads in our apartment over the flower shop next door to the Blue Benn. When I went to look, I found an angel pin that I had given her for her birthday.

Instinctively, Mary Lou pats her right shoulder, as if looking for reassurance that her angel is still in place. "The pin was just sitting there, on top of her jewelry box. That was so strange," she says.

"It felt like a message, that she was always going to be watching over me. So that's why I wear it. Every day. Now it's the two of them, my mom and Sonny, watching over me.

Marcus, Lisa, Bill, Matheson, Mary Lou

CHAPTER THREE

FAMILY

Lisa and Bill LaFlamme

For most of her life, Lisa LaFlamme harbored a love-hate relationship with her parents' business. She celebrated their success, but bristled at the notion of stepping into their shoes. "I was proud of my parents and of the great life they made, but I still grrr — it made me angry," she says just six months after the sale of the business that consumed her parents' lives. Lisa's husband, Bill, walked away from the family firm after a three-year stint in the kitchen, starting a successful window-washing service. Working in a diner, he says firmly, "is not for everyone." It was harder for Lisa to face down the expectations she would build on a beloved legacy. "In the end, it just wasn't me," she says, finally acknowledging the courage it took to say "no" when the world, or at least the town, is hoping you'll say "yes."

Lisa, what was it like growing up in the Blue Benn family?

Lisa: I was 10 when my parents took over the diner. Truthfully, as a kid I was very embarrassed that my parents owned the Blue Benn, because it still took a really long time to turn it around. My parents did amazing things, but it seems like it just took so long for it to get to that.

I went to the old middle school in Bennington, and a minibus would pick me up at the diner and drop me off on Main Street. At the time, it felt like all the other kids took the regular bus; they had siblings; they had some sort of normalcy. My life was a weird —I'm going to school smelling like today's soup and cigarette smoke. Once I asked my father, "Why did you have to pick the restaurant business? And then not give me any siblings to help me sort it out."

I have always compared the diner to a sibling, someone that I have had to compete with most of my life. Yes, I had a really wonderful life, and my parents were always there, but the diner was such a big focus. My parents worked incredibly hard and their success created a monster that ate up all their time.

From an insider's perspective, how did Sonny and Mary Lou balance the diner's workload?

Bill: I think all your father wanted to do was just cook. He really just wanted to concentrate on his recipes and his cooking. He was really in the back of the house, and Mary Lou kind of made everything else work — fixed everything. [*laughs*]

Lisa: Dad was the creative mind behind the diner, but my mother was the force that made it happen. They ran the place with a good cop–bad cop mentality. Mom was the disciplinarian and Dad was the creative guy. He would bitch about things, to me and to my mother and to the family, but never really did anything about it. Mom would have to be the one that would follow through on any issues that needed

Lisa LaFlamme

to be addressed. She was always the one that would have to deal with the crap.

Bill, did you ever consider taking over the diner with Lisa once Mary Lou and Sonny had retired?

Bill: I liked working at the diner at first, probably because it was such a new experience. I didn't realize how frickin' crazy it was and how constantly busy. You hardly had time to go to the bathroom, because it was just always so busy — especially summer and weekends. You get cranky. [*laughs*] Sonny knew I was starting to not like it. He'd come through the backdoor, and he'd look at me, I know he would, and he could see it in my eyes that it wasn't gonna last long. [*laughs*]

I think I could've had the opportunity to get into the family business, but that wasn't what I wanted, And there was friction in the kitchen. Brian [Carpenter] was a much better cook than me. He was a really good cook. Still, I think I may have seemed like a threat to him because I was married to Lisa. He knew all of Sonny's recipes, but he didn't want to share that knowledge. Looking back, I guess I can understand where he was coming from.

Was there ever a time, Lisa, that you thought you'd like to take over the family business?

Lisa: I graduated from [Mount Anthony Union] High School in 1982, and went right to the diner. I had a pretty cushy schedule. My mother never made me open; I could go in at seven in the morning and work until two. Once I got married, I did have more hours because I needed the money, but she always took care of me. I had good hours.

So for a long time, in the early and late eighties, it was fine. I embraced working there; it was fun; my dad and mom were both working there, so it was great. I was an adult, on my own. It turned back around as I took on more responsibility. By that time, a lot of the wait staff had been there for fifteen-plus years and pretty much did what they wanted to do. I'd never been their boss; my mother was always their boss. Brian actually commented to me on that one time. ... I'll own that; I never tried to be their boss. I wanted to be just one of them.

I had begged my mom for years — and my dad, when he was still able to make decisions — I said, please let's cut back the hours. Please. It's too much on everyone. And we were all getting older. I'm the youngest, at — well, I was 56.

Did they ever consider bringing in some new, young waitresses?

Lisa: When you found a home at the Blue Benn, you were there. There were maybe just a handful that ever left or ever got asked to leave. There were waitresses that were there until the end, and had been there practically from the start. I think the longest-serving waitress would've been Brenda: 35 years, probably. And then Jeannie, it was probably not quite 20, maybe. But that's not a huge turnover. Not only that, you know, Pat was my aunt. She was Sonny's sister. So I'm gonna tell her what she's supposed to do and not do? I felt like I could never gain their respect as a boss.

Let's switch gears. Can you tell me one or two of your favorite fun memories of the diner?

Lisa: Going back to the eighties, nineties, there was a guy who came in every morning for breakfast and had the same thing every morning: Cheerios and an English muffin. He used to like annoying the hell out of me — playing the Chipmunks on the jukebox just as he left and yelling "Uh, waitress — waitress!" in an obnoxious voice. So one day, I glued his cereal bowl and spoon to his saucer — stupid, but pretty funny. I think he switched to eggs after that.

And there was the belly dancer. There was a dentist in town who was kind of prankster. His staff got him back on his birthday. They asked for our permission first, because he came into the diner early every morning, between six and seven. We were all for it. They had hired a belly dancer to come in and perform. Not a glamorous belly dancer. So he's sitting in the last booth on the right-hand side where he always sat and she comes in. She had her music and her little cymbals and her little outfit and she starts doing her thing. We just stood back and watched his face get redder and redder and redder. It didn't last for more than a few minutes, but what a show. It was funny.

And favorite childhood memories with your parents?

Lisa: My mom had a certain day off during the week, I think it was on Wednesday nights. The two of us would go to Howard Johnson's together and have a date night. That was special. I got to work with my dad mornings, and that was nice. I wish that I had paid better attention to my father's talent over the years. I wish I'd paid more attention to him in the kitchen.

I love that the boys, especially Matheson, learned to cook with my father. From middle school, he started going in and working with my dad in the kitchen. So he made the menu quite early with his chocolate chip and raspberry pancakes. Marcus made the menu much later — bacon-apple-cheddar omelet.

Bill LaFlamme

Generations

Bill: Sonny had good times with the two boys. The three of them, they did hang out. They'd go for walks, over the Blue Trail, and he'd play with them when they were small, mostly when like six to twelve. And then the boys started playing sports, and Sonny wasn't into sports, so — not knocking Sonny, but it just wasn't his thing. It was Mary Lou who went to all the games.

Did the family file away all of Sonny's recipes?

Lisa: For years and years, we tried to talk him into writing a cookbook; just writing down some things. He was like, "Oh, yeah, maybe." ... In the end, he never did. He would write some things down on pieces of paper, put it in a notebook and stash it in the reach-in cooler. Because he's pretty much been out of the diner for the last 10 years, I asked my mom if she knew where he put that notebook. "Just give me some time" was her answer. I don't want to pressure her about it.

Of course, I know a few. The crunchberry pancakes — that's just granola and raspberries in the batter. [*laughs*] The nutburger. ... So here's what my dad said to a customer one time, about the nutburger. She asked what held it together. And he told her, peanut butter. And that was totally untrue. He just did not want her to know what went in that nutburger. So I guess we'll leave it at that. [*Cheshire cat smile*]

Now that the diner has been sold, how does it feel to no longer have it in your life?

Lisa: I say I hated the place, that I had a love-hate relationship with it. But then I think about the people I met there. So many of my customers made me feel so special, when they would come in the diner. There were just a lot of really nice people that loved the place. These are people I wouldn't have ever met, if not for the diner. But my happiest times were when Dad was there.

Bill: The Blue Benn has been in our lives since we got together. There've been ups and downs, pros and cons. But watching our kids grow up through that diner, from here to where they are now — you know, working in the kitchen, playing the jukebox, bringing their girlfriends and their friends — so it was fun to see. It was fun to be a part of that.

"But my happiest times were when Dad was there."
— Lisa LaFlamme

patagonia

Matheson and Marcus LaFlamme

For most of their lives, the LaFlamme brothers were seen as the obvious heirs to the town's favorite dining legacy. Matheson was in the kitchen with his grandfather as far back as he can remember. His first lesson was in how to make a roux, that frothy mix of flour and butter that forms the base of dozens of delicious dishes. Marcus was more a "front-of-the-house kind of guy," who in high school learned from his grandmother how to keep the Blue Benn's books. They both loved the diner, the ambience, the camaraderie and the slightly absurd sense of celebrity they'd enjoy whenever they took a few friends or a date there to eat. But both boys had their hearts set on discovering a bigger world than Bennington, Vermont, and on forging different lives from those of their grandparents. They look back on the restaurant with great fondness, a hint of nostalgia, and an abundance of pride to be part of a family tradition that brought joy to a community hungry for conversation and connection, with a side order of hearty food.

Marcus: I'm the youngest of the grandchildren, I'm 24. I graduated from Mount Anthony High School and then I went to the University of Hartford, in Connecticut, where I majored in political science. I have a minor in sociology, but I don't tell anyone that. [*laughs*] As of lately, I've been interested in real estate, so I've been studying to become a real estate agent.

Matheson: I also went to Mount Anthony and studied finance at Western New England University in Springfield. I wanted to become a financial advisor, so I moved to Connecticut and got a job in wealth management with a small firm, right after college; studied for my CFP — certified financial planner. I passed the test, became a CFP, and then I decided I wanted to get into sales. [*laughs*] So, complete shift.

One of our firm's largest clients was a partner at a large insurance agency in West Hartford, and he took me on as his protégé. So I was there for three years — I actually just resigned last week — and I just took a new job in Manhattan for a pretty large brokerage, USI Insurance Services, focusing on real estate. I'll be on the train on Monday.

Marcus: I never really had that much of an interest in owning the diner. Sure, when I was younger, it was always the greatest place to be and I guess it crossed my mind, what if? But I was never that much involved in cooking, not like Matheson. When I worked there, I only dish-washed and bussed tables — Matheson was on the grill.

For me it was always great going into the Blue Benn. I have lots of great memories of the place. I never really wanted to take it over, but at the same time I never felt angry or discouraged by it.

Matheson: Nobody in the family ever suggested my brother or I take over the diner; people outside of the family did, a lot. But, like Marcus said, I don't think either of us wanted to grow roots here. I think we both wanted to get out of the area. I never considered taking over the diner, but when I was younger, and learning about cooking from grandpa, I was set on going to culinary school. I realized pretty quickly it's a lot of work and a lot of pressure. [*laughs*] I guess I realized it just wasn't the right career path for me.

Gordon Ramsay used to be my idol. But even the top chefs will work eighteen-hour days, which is fine, but for most chefs, the pay is typically not there. Luckily, I saw that early, and I was like, no, I'm not going to do that; I'm not gonna sign myself up for that. But I do enjoy cooking now, a lot. I have a small army of cookbooks at home. [*laughs*]

Marcus: I did work there in the summers; I also worked there during the school year, as well, because I had a field-study class on the Blue Benn. [*laughs*] We both had classes on the Blue Benn. [*laughter*]

Mount Anthony encouraged internships, which they called field study. We both decided to learn more of the business from our grandma. So she would teach us the books. Our lessons were more oriented toward the financial component of the business. We helped with the payroll, all of the reports that she would run. There was a bit of financial analysis, you know; margins are very thin in that industry.

Matheson: I actually started working at the Blue Benn when I was young, way before high school. I think how it started was that we had to do community service, at Sacred Heart Elementary School, so I just worked at the diner. [*laughs*] I would go in with my dad at like two o'clock in the morning and prep.

He did it to give Brian a day off on Saturday and did not like it. But I liked it. I liked getting up. I liked cooking. I tried to teach myself and create my own dishes. I was working with Poppy, my grandpa, too. He actually went in earlier than my dad; when he worked, he would go in at 10 o'clock at night and work until like eight or nine in the morning.

The first thing my grandpa taught me was how to make a roux, which is a way of thickening sauces. It's what a sous chef would learn in France where the cuisine is all about sauce.

When I was really into cooking, my grandpa asked one of our food service providers, US Foods, to give us a tour of their facility in Saratoga Springs, New York. So me, my grandpa, and Brian Carpenter [the Blue Benn cook] drove all the way out there for a tour and a special lesson from their in-house cook. It was a lot of fun, and eye-opening, for somebody so young. I was only about 10 or 11.

Marcus: It's funny, but looking back I wish I'd learned about cooking in the diner. I do regret that. I'm a few years younger than Matheson and he was already pretty young to be getting into the whole diner scene.

I would've been five when my dad started his window-cleaning business. Typically, he would just work Saturdays at the diner. He never was full-time, that I can remember. I know my dad really wanted me to window-clean with him. [*laughs*]

I window-cleaned with my dad a few summers ... so mostly I spent summer job time with him. [*laughs*]

Matheson: Marcus was a natural in the front of the house. He's a very good personality, he's great with people, and he can definitely command a room. So his place in a restaurant would definitely be in the front of the house, directly interacting with customers.

A Few Blue Benn Stats

- Donuts consumed in a day: 27
- Number of omelets on the menu: 18
- Eggs cooked on a Saturday: 50 dozen
- Orders served on a busy day: 500
- Times "Moonlight in Vermont" was played when Mary Lou and Sonny ran the diner: 10 times a week, and even more when the leaf peepers showed up.

Marcus: I just waited on a couple customers, just taking a couple orders. I never did it full-on. My mom always encouraged me; a lot of people encouraged me to, and I said it just wasn't for me. I didn't want to take from the waitresses, either — it's a small diner to share customers with too many wait staff.

Matheson: As for cooking, I think I took to it naturally. I really enjoyed it. And, this may seem weird, but I really enjoyed the pressure of being on the line. I really relished that, even from a young age, which is very odd. I guess the pressure was exciting. You had to think through every step. So, for example, you're making omelets, using spices. As soon as one comes out of the pan, you have to clean out the pan, get rid of any trace of spice. It was as if you always had to think a few steps ahead. You have to plan what components of whatever you're making and prepare them in what sequence: throwing stuff in the microwave, throwing stuff on the grill; timing when you put the eggs in; what do you have in the oven; what do you have under the broiler. You're multitasking all over the place.

I definitely learned most of it from my grandpa, and maybe a little from my dad. But, again, he hated working in the kitchen. [*laughs*]

Marcus: It was interesting, to work the front of the house, because every time I was in there, or Matheson was in there, we would recognize somebody. That was the Blue Benn, we always knew one of the customers and sometimes, we just knew everyone. It was a great place to run into people, I'll tell you that.

In the kitchen

Bumpersticker

It definitely had a family atmosphere, a sense of community. It was also touristy, which I think was a good combination. People would come from all over to visit. They'd want to visit the Blue Benn, which gave it a whole other status. And then there was the community of waitresses and the staff, and their relationships with the customers. Those relationships last forever.

Matheson: I don't think there's any other place in the area where you would get that communal feel. I can't really think of anywhere. I'm not just saying that because of our attachment to the diner, but I genuinely can't think of anywhere else.

I put it down to the way that our grandparents conducted themselves and the way the staff developed relationships with customers. It's also about the sheer amount of time that they ran that diner. It's just been around for so long and it's been such a part of the community — a real Bennington institution.

Marcus: My grandparents put a lot of hard work into it. They really transformed that place.

Matheson: That's so true and it's funny because to us it seemed like our grandpa had only had one pace: slow [*laughter*]. That was true whether he was walking or driving or cooking.

Marcus: [*laughs*] He made up for it in the diner, though.

Matheson: Absolutely, especially when he worked the line in the morning. When he was there, he would definitely get a ton of orders at one time. But he never pushed people or got tough or went all Gordon Ramsay in the kitchen. [*laughs*] He actually really did not like Gordon Ramsay at all. I would say he was more methodical about what he did, but he didn't really push anybody. I don't think he ever yelled at anybody, honestly. That was my grandma's job. She was the enforcer. Except with us. With us she's never been anything but supportive and kind.

Marcus: Yeah, that's true. [*laughs*]

Matheson: It's tough to find somebody in the restaurant industry with our [grandfather] Poppy's demeanor.

Thinking about Gordon Ramsay, I remember I had a Gordon Ramsay cookbook when I was about 10 years old. [*laughs*] There was this brioche French toast recipe in it that I really wanted to make. So Poppy and I made a morning of it, prepping the fresh peaches and working out the recipe. That's probably the first thing that we made together and the start of when I began working at the diner. It went really well, too. People liked it.

Looking back, I don't think most people would allow a 10-year-old to work up a new recipe in a kitchen prepping for the morning breakfast crowd. [*laughs*]

Marcus: It's funny how my friends still talk about going to the Blue Benn. ... It's like a giant, important memory for them, like they went to an amazing ballgame.

Matheson: [*laughs*] There was a certain cachet to being related to the owners. We took pride in telling the history of the diner and sharing our experiences there. Our friends enjoyed hearing that; hopefully, they did. [*laughs*] And the food's really good, too; that doesn't hurt. People legitimately enjoyed it, especially, the breakfast burrito. My friends loved the breakfast burrito.

Marcus: I don't think we had any birthday parties there; it's a little small there, I guess. But we did have pasta dinners there for soccer. The whole team would be there the night before the game. We had probably twenty-two of us — in booths and sitting at the counter.

Matheson: It was fun and it was pretty funny to see, too.

Marcus: One perk we didn't get was cutting the line. [*laughs*] No way. A lot of people won't go to the counter if there are open seats. So if there were four people waiting, three counter seats, my brother and I could get in, no problem.

Matheson: Pop right in there.

Marcus: But go to the booths? Forget it. We never even tried to go to the booths, really, unless we had some friends that we wanted to show the Blue Benn for the first time; we might use a booth.

Matheson: Yeah, that's true.

Marcus: Or we were with the ladies or something. [*laughter*] I've taken girls there I liked and never wound up

Matheson and Lisa

Poppy and his grandsons, circa 2000s

dating. But if I really had a crush on a girl, I'd take her to the Blue Benn. Yep, I've been on many Blue Benn dates.

Matheson: [*laughs*]

Marcus: But I knew not to go when my mom was working.

Matheson: Too many mom questions. [*laughs*] And there were the menu items named after us. Actually, we both created our own dishes and grandma put them on the menu with our names.

I was in fifth grade. That clearly sticks out in my mind. And it was Valentine's Day weekend. I really wanted to create my own thing. I was getting the creative juices flowing, and everything I saw around that time of year had chocolate and raspberry in it. So I thought let's make a pancake with those ingredients — [*laughs*] chocolate chips and raspberries. Not the most creative thing in the world, but they went over very well. They sold very, very well.

Marcus: Mine was a bacon and apple and cheddar omelet.

Matheson: That's more creative than chocolate chips and raspberries.

Marcus: Eh, I don't know. I've heard mixed reviews on mine. But I'm glad that finally made it onto the menu, after years of not having my own item. [*laughs*] I really wanted a menu item because everyone loved Matheson's dish. They'd always ask, "Marcus, where's your dish?" Where's yours? For years.

Matheson: [*laughs*] Typical little brother reaction. I used to tell people that I got a monthly royalty check for it. [*laughs*]

Marcus: Feelings about the sale? In a way it's a relief for the family to have the decision made — less to worry about. And now people can stop hounding us if we're ever gonna take it over. [*laughs*] But it also it's sad to see it go. It's an iconic institution in this town. My brother and I spent hours and hours of our lives there. The diner has been in our family ever since we were born.

Matheson: When Poppy got sick, it became so tough for my grandma to manage the diner, even with my mom. I think at that point, she just wanted to be done with it, but she kept on because she thought he would have wanted her to. When Covid hit, it gave her an exit strategy. I think she realized it was time to end that chapter and move on.

New awnings, circa 1990

COOKING WITH YOUR HEART & SOUL

Excerpts from a high school essay by Matheson LaFlamme

Matheson writes his 10th grade Honors English essay, "Backstage at Bennington's Blue Benn," as a character based largely on the Blue Benn's head chef, Brian Carpenter. Excerpts follow:

Sonny and I started at the Vermont Restaurant, and that is where our culinary knowledge came from. During our time at the Vermont Restaurant, Sonny married Mary Lou in 1962. Mary Lou would play an equally important role at the diner as Sonny. … Sonny left [the Vermont Restaurant] to work at the Blue Benn in 1973. I continued working there, but not for long.

When Sonny took over the diner, he offered me the job as cook because of our friendship and my restaurant experience. At the time, Sonny, Mary Lou, Randy Webber and I were the only employees.

I remember my first day at the Blue Benn. … I walked into such a different culinary world; it presents such a different atmosphere and experience compared to any other restaurant. … Diners are sort of their own breed. … It doesn't matter who is in the diner, everyone there is like family. The homestyle food reinforces this, and the tight and cramped booths and incredibly small stools reinforce this. Other restaurants just cannot create this atmosphere and attitude.

When I started out at the diner, I was overwhelmed by the size of the menu. … There are 18 different omelets available alone! Many cooks have come and gone; the menu is intricate and mind-boggling. People have told me that the Blue Benn is the most challenging restaurant that they ever worked in because there are simply so many dishes. … The "breakfast rush" was especially challenging; the sheer rate at which you have to put out orders is insane. When Sonny realized I could not handle it all on the first day, he made me peel potatoes. … Every time I would use the peeler, it would slice the potato and slice my skin. I could not wait for the day to end. I wanted to cook with Sonny. … I was inspired and awed by the menu.

The Blue Benn has a high number of homemade foods. Items such as donuts, pies, cinnamon buns and "specialty" pancakes are homemade. All meats are roasted and a [40-pound] turkey is roasted every morning. Sonny also uses his own vegetables from his garden whenever he can. When I make homemade food it's like making a connection with the diner and the customers because the food is so genuine. It really is like cooking with your heart and soul.

It isn't just about the food for me, it's about how people enjoy the experience of the diner. Mary Lou and Sonny have worked incredibly hard for over 35 years … and their hard work has certainly come to fruition. … I am proud to say I have worked for this culinary heaven and seen and talked to so many interesting people that have passed through here.

Laurie Harrington and Jean Andrew

Ben Roth

Wake up, Bennington!

Fran York rushes the piping hot coffee and O.J. to early morning breakfast customers at the Blue Benn Diner. For pictures and story of earning mornings at the diner see page 5.

Bennington Banner

Weekly founded 1841, Daily 1903

Bennington, Vermont | Saturday, November 7, 1981 | 25 Cents

Reagan stresses need to keep cutting

NEW YORK (AP) — President Reagan promised the party faithful Friday night that he is "not retreating one inch" from his economic program and will keep asking Congress to cut spending rather than raise taxes.

In toughly worded remarks to a $1,000-a-person fund-raiser at the Waldorf-Astoria hotel, Reagan suggested his critics may actually be "rooting for recession and misery on Main Street."

But he insisted he will stick with his program despite new figures that show he is losing ground in the battle to balance the budget by 1984.

Record high interest rates and an unexpectedly swift decline in inflation have cost the government revenues, Reagan said. But that won't "cause us to push the panic button."

"We're going to keep on asking the Congress for more spending cuts until we get government costs down to within government revenues. Maybe it'll take a little longer than we planned, but we're not retreating one inch."

Dismissing suggestions that he would bow to congressional pressure and increase taxes instead of making further cuts in federal programs, Reagan said, "We made a commitment to the American people and we're going to keep it. Your tax reduction will not be rescinded; it will not be delayed; and it will not be reduced."

"We didn't select our program because it would be easy or quick or politically expedient ... we are here to lead the struggle to save our economy. This is our moment."

Reagan's unexpectedly strong rhetoric came on the heels of a day of meetings with Republican leaders from the House and Senate, many of whom urged him to call for tax increases in 1983 and 1984 to counteract declining revenues and the increased costs of the current recession.

But Reagan told the fund-raiser, "we came to Washington with a plan. The plan is on track even though the train is a little late leaving the station."

But despite statements by aides that the president opposes large tax hikes to shrink recession-swelled deficits, congressional sources insisted they believed Reagan might still consider up to $45 billion in hikes in 1983 and 1984.

That would be twice as large as the $22 billion, three-year plan he called for in September, but far less than the $84 billion plan advanced by some Senate Republicans.

Reagan's spokesman said the president "would at least entertain" proposals for higher taxes at a later date if they appear necessary.

"I do not want to see any change" in the tax cuts Congress already has passed, a spokesman quoted Reagan as saying at a White House meeting with congressional Republicans.

"Nor do I wish to see any tax increases," the spokesman, Larry Speakes, quoted Reagan as saying. "He does not look with favor on tax increases in 1983 and 1984," Speakes said.

But Senate Republicans emerging from the White House said Reagan might be receptive to tax increases in 1983 and 1984 beyond an earlier request.

"In my opinion the president is willing to consider future revenue enhancements in 1983 and 1984 of a significant nature," Senate Republican Leader Howard Baker Jr. of Tennessee said.

Speakes later told reporters that Baker had a "correct impression." He said the president "is willing to entertain what has become known as revenue enhancement," namely tax increases, although his preference would be spending cuts.

Treasury Secretary Donald T. Regan said the president told the congressional delegation that "with the change in the economic climate and the changing taking place in spending and the like, we probably will not be able to achieve a balanced budget in 1984."

But Regan said the president "insisted that we had to be on a path that would lead toward a balanced budget ... as quickly as possible."

As for balancing the budget in 1984, Reagan said, "We're going in that direction. I never said anything but that it was a goal. The eventual goal, whether it comes then or whether it has to be delayed or not, is a balanced budget."

At the same time, he conceded there have been "changes in the estimates" of economic performance in recent weeks. And Baker and Pete V. Domenici, R-N.M., chairman of the Senate Budget Committee both said later the deficit this year could be $80 billion.

6,000 GIs will be sent on Mideast maneuvers

Fran York, Bennington Banner, November 7, 1981

CHAPTER FOUR

STAFF

Blue Benn
DINER
HOT CHILI SAUCE
Blue Benn
DINER

Heidi Tilley

The girls used to call me the 'mean waitress'," shaking her head, Heidi laughs. "It was part of our act. I'd be going, well, you guys are the only ones who think I'm mean. My customers love me." In 2001 Heidi had hoped to celebrate 23 years working at Sonny's Blue Benn, but life changed when the state government, battling to contain the Covid pandemic, shut down bars and restaurants all across Vermont. Married with two kids, Heidi started waitressing at 19, her first job at a diner in Chester. She soon came home to Bennington and eventually went to work for Mary Lou and Sonny. At 60, her infamous disposition was long ago revealed: sweet and sour in equal measure.

When I went looking for a job at the Blue Benn, I talked to Mary Lou for just a few minutes. She knew me from when I worked at the Paradise Motel and from when I was a kid and she worked with my father at Polygraphic over in North Bennington. So she said to come in and basically do a one-day training. After that, I did dishes, I cleared tables, and I worked whatever times she had open for a waitress — mostly it would be late morning through lunch or Wednesday night dinner. I worked whatever hours I could get, but it's the weekends, when there's no time to eat and you're grabbing a cup of soup or a muffin or whatever, when you make money. Those are the shifts you want. And I'll tell you, it was hardest fucking job I've ever had waitressing.

Menu board, 2021

There's so much stuff on the menu. You had to know what goes with what and once you did, Sonny'd come up with another dish or two. It's not just the whole five-page menu thrown at you, but you had your breakfast items, your luncheon items, you had vegetarian items and the dinner stuff. All that stuff — you just had to learn everything from serving it and seeing it on the plate.

The first week I was there I'd go home and I'd just be in tears. I'd go, do I really have to go back? Because it was just so busy and so fast. But after a while it was great. Sure, it was a job. But I liked my job. I really liked my job.

It's a ballet. Behind the counter, in the kitchen, passing each other with food in our hands. It looks effortless, like ballet. And then there's another dance with the customers. You try to read your customers. Some people can come in and you know they're in a shitty mood, so I try to make that go away. I try to change their mood before they leave. I'm a little sarcastic, I know I am, but not mean sarcastic, you know. I liked the people that came in and I wanted them to leave feeling good.

People went there partly for the food — like I said, it's a diner and the food is good — but mostly they came because the experience of the place is really fun. It's kind of like stepping into a time warp.

The music never changes. Once in a while we'd get a new song on the juke box, but not very often. The same father-son team still services the juke boxes, although now it's mostly the son. The music is from the fifties and sixties. The older stuff 'cause you've got to make everybody happy.

Sometimes I 'd have customers dancing in the aisles. I one time had a customer come in on Valentine's Day. It was pretty empty; most people go to fancy restaurants that night. But this guy came in with candles and they played a bunch of old songs and got up and started slow dancing in the aisle. They were probably in their sixties. It was nice. We turned down the main lights and just left the upper lights on so it would be sort romantic.

[See Bill and Cinda Morse's interview on page 87 for the couple's version of the story].

We even had a few proposals in there.

Sonny was always in a good mood. He was just teasing everybody all the time.

And we all ran with it. We'd go with whatever he said and then just keep it up.

Sonny would start to tease Brenda about her dating. He'd tell her every time she dated a customer we'd lose a customer. We'd get in on it and tease her about breaking up with guys and that we were gonna lose all our customers if she wasn't careful. That kinda stuff.

In all the years I've been there with Sonny and Mary Lou, it was always MaryLou who would give you a talking to. She'd have a little chat with you, and hopefully everything worked out and you'd listen to what she said. I've been talked to in that back booth I think just once. Everybody has. Once, Brian and I got — Brian said something to me and I just got pissed, and it got a little out of control. So Mary Lou took us outside by ourselves and told us we'd better work it out. And we did. Brian and I have worked together since Brian was fourteen, when he was a dish washer at the Paradise. The thing about it is, remembering that time makes me realize all over again what a good boss she was. Instead of saying, you know, you're out of here she gave us both a chance to make it right.

At the end of the day, it's a job, but Sonny and Mary Lou are the best people that I've ever worked for in all the years that I've waitressed. They treat their employees really well. They pay you more than waitress pay. Mary Lou is by the book on everything, so you're allowed sick pay. So if you don't use your hours for sickness at the end of the year you get a check from her for all your sick pay. No other restaurant that I know of anywhere does that for their employees. They're just nice. We all got paid vacations. Never had a paid vacation. And on top of that, they were always fun to work with. I'd still be working there if they weren't closed down.*

When the state closed restaurants down, Mary Lou sent us all letters. At first, I didn't feel like that was a good thing to do. I thought she could have told us in person, but I think it was just too hard for her to face everybody. I understand that. People keep telling me to go get a job. I don't want any job. I want to like what I'm doing. I guess we were all a little spoiled working in the Benn for so long.

** Heidi has returned to work at the Blue Benn under new ownership.*

Eggs and Pancakes
Jim Woodward

Bill Walsh

At 55, Bill Walsh could pass for a roadie in a rock 'n' roll band or the leader of a motorcycle gang. He's neither, but the ink on his forearms and the Icarus tattoo on his neck — the mythic figure whose waxed wings melted when he flew too close to the sun — speak of hard living and adventure. Bill held a slew of jobs before landing at the Blue Benn, from managing the seafood department at Price Chopper to working as the head cook in a Bennington steakhouse. The past 21 years have been spent working for Mary Lou and Sonny.

I remember my dad telling me when I was a kid, "What do you wanna do, work in a greasy spoon all your life?" I bring that up to him a lot because I did end up working in a greasy spoon for a good portion of my life.

Sonny'd come in to the steakhouse and he'd see me working in there by myself with the place packed. He wanted me. I got a phone call from him when I'd already agreed to the job at Price Chopper. He said, "There's an opening finally. Could you please come in?" I said, "Sonny, I just started a career. I'll give you my days off and I'll help you that way." That's how I started at the Blue Benn, as a part-time person. It was a good fit and I liked it, but it was tough. In the winter, I would work probably 58 hours a week, 60. In the summer, it was pushing 70, a little over 70 sometimes.

People don't realize the diner has a downstairs that

runs its whole length with four or five rooms down there. Walk-in freezer, walk-in cooler, storerooms, rooms with mixers and blenders. It was cellar-y, very dank, but good enough. When I'd go down there, I'd always look at Sonny and go, "You need anything?" He goes, "Nothing you can get." He always, always, always had a way of making you smile just by some line he would come out with.

Sonny had a lot of tricks. The way he flowed through a kitchen, it was almost mythical. The only thing about Sonny that I could joke about him is he dirtied every single thing in the place. When a dishwasher came in after Sonny had worked, it was a nightmare for them, but he had a grace and an elegance in the kitchen. That's maybe something I picked up from him, the ability to do seven to ten things at a time. Sonny would be doing one thing and then he'd walk to the next thing and he'd walk over to the next thing, and everything was going at the same time. Everything was perfect when he was done. Everything was perfect. He didn't lose one thing for the other. He had his method perfectly entrenched into his movements.

He was that good. Brian [Carpenter, head cook] learned specifically from Sonny. Sonny would go in around two in the morning. That's when he would begin his shift. He would work until we opened. He'd stay a little while and then he'd get out of there. He was into it when there was nobody there. I'm sure in the beginning of his career, he was out there hobnobbing with everybody. Toward the end, he didn't really particularly care for the crowds. He would shy away from them. He'd seen it, done it, and he was – well. I think he just wanted to go home.

He loved his garden. He had a massive garden that we used to source when we could in the diner. He grew all kinds of stuff. His dad was heavily into gardening, too. It was something that they shared together. His dad lived in the same property area.

The Blue Benn is a stressful cooking atmosphere. Many a high-level cook would come there and pretty much run, tell us they couldn't do it. I've seen men start crying in the kitchen. The orders come in rapid fire. The waitresses are reading check nine and you're on check three. But even reading the slips, that wasn't easy. Don't get me started on the handwriting and they're on this grease-soaked counter and you can barely make out the order with the grease soaking into the paper. Meantime you're rushing to get the food out. Like I said, you're in a fast, speed-orientated situation.

But cooking with Sonny? That was a treat. It was like standing next to a teacher. My motto in the kitchen is that there are no rules in cooking. I'm pretty sure I picked that up from Sonny. When he was done with what he was doing, it was always pretty near perfect

"But cooking with Sonny? That was a treat. It was like standing next to a teacher. My motto in the kitchen is that there are no rules in cooking. I'm pretty sure I picked that up from Sonny."

— Bill Walsh

At the grill

Jim Woodward

Silk City Diner tag 4815. The Blue Benn was the 15th diner manufactured in 1948.

looking. It's hard not to pick up on something like that. He had a touch to everything he did. He would experiment sometimes. We'd be like, "I don't know." But sure enough, it was a success. He had the run of the diner. It was his diner.

As for Mary Lou, I've never met anyone like her. She was just – a heart of gold.

People would ask me, is there much that scares you? I'd say Mary Lou's glare. When you were on her radar, oh boy. I'm a hard horse to corral and I was constantly in her wheelhouse when I first got to the diner. After a while she figured me out and I figured her out and we came to an understanding.

When you picked up your paycheck and it was thick, your gut just dropped right down to your knees. You knew it wasn't good. It would always start out, "William." I knew something I did, did not please her. I always read it with very meticulous care and tried my best to not duplicate that thing again.

I'm so proud to have worked there. When Mary Lou sent me that final letter, telling us she'd decided to close, she opened it up with "This is the hardest letter I've ever written in my life." I could almost feel her through that letter. Her heartstrings were in that pen.

I've never worked for anyone like those two. Always there to help anybody. I remember we had a couple really dirtbag dishwashers. I hate to say that word, but it turned out to be true. Mary Lou tried so hard to help them. When they were down and out, she'd lend 'em money or she'd get 'em something. Heart of gold. Sonny was a heart of a gold in his nature, but he didn't personally involve himself with any of us. He left that to Mary Lou. That was how they balanced out the work. They were perfect for each other.

Brenda Eggsware

Laughing, Brenda Eggsware remembers the day when a rowdy foursome at one of the Blue Benn's booths cranked up "Sweet Caroline" on the jukebox. They started singing, and the next booth joined in, and before the waitresses could serve up a fresh mug of coffee, the whole place was chanting "Sweet Caroline, good times never seemed so good. ..." Unable to resist, a few started dancing in the aisle, leaving the waitresses pressed against the counter as they watched, astonished. "That was how it was sometimes. Special," Brenda says, looking back over the 30 years she worked there. Her last day came on St Patrick's Day, March 17, 2020. "By then, things were real slow and going south fast. Covid was the end of it all." Soon after the Benn closed, Brenda, 61, moved to Indiana to be near her daughter.

I started working at the Benn in 1981 and stayed there until March 17, 2020. I was working at CB Sports back then. I was one of their fastest sewers, but they had started sending stuff overseas [for stitching]. I was making less than half of what I used to make and I had three small children. That's why I started looking for another job. One day, Lisa [Monroe] — she was married to my brother — picked me up and she goes, "I hear you're lookin' for a job. Come work for my parents!" I said "Oh my god, I never waitressed before, I couldn't do that." She kept saying, just come talk to my mom. So I met Mary Lou at the diner and we talk and she

says Brenda, "I'll be there every minute, you don't have to worry."

My first two weeks at the Benn, I cried. A lot. The first day I was absolutely petrified, but Mary Lou was right there. She was very methodical about training a waitress. She didn't just throw you to the wolves. She started me off slow with a couple of counter customers or maybe a table. She knew what she was doing. She's a great boss. And she was funny! She could really throw some corkers out there.

When I first started, I'd open Thursday, Friday and Saturday mornings and I would come in later Monday mornings at around seven. I'd set up both sides of the diner, put on the hot water and suds, get the dishwasher set up, a lot of stocking, put the specials up for the day. Sometimes I'd be hustling for a good hour trying to get everything done … then the other person would arrive at six.

Sonny always worked mornings, that's how I got to know him so well. Mary Lou used to be in there a lot in the mornings too. I'd come in at five in the morning and Sonny would be in there with the jukebox blaring. He loved swing and jazz, the old songs. It kept him going. He'd get there at one or two in the morning every day and start cooking and working on his recipes. A lot of times I'd be the only one in there with him and we'd have a good laugh.

I worked with Sonny for 20 years before he retired. All those years, I got used to the wisecracking. We'd get each other laughing so hard, we'd have tears in our eyes. We really did. I loved working with him. It didn't seem like a job half the time 'cause you'd go in the kitchen and he'd be joking around, teasing everybody. Sometimes the job could be stressful, especially for Sonny, and you have to make fun of things. He worked really hard and I think that's why he joked around so much. You have to have that release and I think it was the same thing with us girls.

There was a group of us that got used to his banter, we were kind of inspired by it. I worked with his sister Pat a lot and she'd slap me on the bottom, call me silly names, funny stuff like that. You get to know each other, then you'd make fun of each other and get the customers in on it. It was all good fun. There were a couple of the girls who'd egg on the customers as well. I'd tease them a bit, if I thought they could handle it, but I'd let on fast that I was kidding and they'd just think it was hysterical. You couldn't help but have a good time in the diner. It put people in a good mood.

Of course, there were sad days. I'll never forget 9/11. I was working that day, still married at the time. My husband called me and said a plane hit one of the World Trade Center towers. I was working with Pat at the time, I think it was a Tuesday. Then he calls back and says Brenda, a plane just hit the second tower. I went "Oh my god, World War III, it's World War III." I came out from the kitchen and I started crying. I said another plane just hit the other tower and all the customers, everyone got really quiet. I think it was shock.

* * *

It was the food that [drew people to the Benn] and the atmosphere. It was so special. The juke boxes would be playin' old songs and we'd have times when someone would get up and start dancin' in the aisle.

The funny thing is it didn't really matter who you were in there and you could never tell who was who. I remember one time, a guy left me a $30 tip and I said to the other girls, I don't think they meant to do that. So I go running out of the diner shouting you left too much! He laughed and said, "No, we meant to do that." He coulda been a celebrity. We sure got our share of celebrities.

Like I've told Mary Lou so many times, you know, you spoiled us. They made it easy to work for them. One of my very best memories was when they threw me a surprise party to celebrate 25 years working in the diner with a huge cake and 25 roses. It was just so sweet. That was how Mary Lou was, she always took care of us. Sometimes I'd come in all teary eyed when I was goin' through my divorce and she'd hug me. I went through a lot years ago and she'd always be there.

Brenda and Jeff Dressler

For a moment, Brenda pauses and leans back from the small wooden table where we're seated. We've met at a local café, sipping coffee outdoors, as fiery autumn leaves swirl around us. Picking up her empty cup — black, no sugar—she smiles, and crisply sums up 30 years as a waitress in Mary Lou and Sonny's diner:

Working at the Blue Benn made me a better person.

Dot Weeks, Frieda Gardner, Chris Percey, Jeff Kinney

Eileen Main

At 18 years old, Eileen Main was juggling three jobs and coolly handling the multiple pressures of work. It was the day-to-day challenges she found flummoxing. "I was a kid playing at being a grown-up," Eileen says, illustrating her case with a story of buying her first car: an $8,000 Volkswagen Fox, paid for in cash "stuffed away" from her waitress gig at Sonny's Blue Benn. Papers signed, she asked the dealer, what next? "I had just bought a car! In my mind, I thought they should take me to dinner, or something." The dealer must have looked baffled. "So I ask him, do I get a meal, or what?" Amused enough to play along, he took her to a nearby Rutland diner. Back the next day to pick up her car, she drove it in second gear the whole way home to Bennington. She'd never driven a stick shift, never owned a car and never been more than 100 miles from home. Life was just starting.

I'm 52, today, actually, it's my birthday. I've lived in Bennington my entire life. My family owned a retail paint and wallpaper store here since I was in fifth grade. I worked in nearly every store downtown, and so did my sister, and my brother. I didn't go to college. Although in high school I was definitely college prep, but I came from people that didn't go to college. Their thinking was if you have ambition, you'll make it.

Actually, I was supposed to go to college. My parents didn't really want me to; they didn't have the money, and I didn't have that much money, but I thought, I gotta do something. So I applied to go to college, without any idea of what I was going for. The week that I graduated from high school, I was at the Blue Benn, and Sonny and Mary Lou's niece was working. We got talking and she tells me they're looking for a waitress. She's like, "They make amazing money." I'd worked at every story downtown, but I'd never waitressed. I'll tell you about retail, it's a special kind of hell. You don't make any money, but you work all the time. So she got me thinking.

I figured I was still gonna go to college. I was just

Detail of logo created by Lon Wasco, 1995

gonna work for the summer at the Blue Benn. Mary Lou knew my parents from the paint store, so she hired me, because she knew that I was responsible. I was lucky because they were super picky about who could work there. That was 1987.

So I get the job at the Blue Benn, and I make so much money, and I'd never made money like that. Remember this is 1987 and we're making minimum wage, around $3.22 an hour. I worked about 20 hours a week — my paycheck was like $63 — but I would make at least $500 a week. It was amazing. I just stuffed it all in the bank.

The $63 paycheck was kind of a joke; the waitresses would forget to pick them up. Well, at least Tracy, Mary Lou's niece, and I did. I'm sure the other ladies didn't forget. We were 18 and pretty clueless, just girls happy to have cash to buy clothes and stuff. But the old-timers, those women had families and kids to support. They were worried we were gonna let somebody know how much money we made. [*laughs*]

I was so happy to be making that kind of money that I decided not to go to college. I was like, you know what? I want to make some money. I didn't know what I wanted to do — all my friends were ready to go to college, and my parents, it was just not on their radar. Even though I'd sent the deposit money in, my parents didn't even know where it was and I didn't go visiting. There was no enthusiasm for the idea from anyone, including myself.

I lived with my parents on Silver Street in Bennington, up at the top of the hill. I worked only one morning shift, sometimes two — my normal shift was two to eight. The morning shift was the money shift. So when I had to work a morning shift, I was a nervous wreck, because I'm a night owl. I'd rather just stay up all night than wake up at four-thirty in the morning. To wake up I'd walk to work, which is kind of a weird hour for your 18-year-old daughter to be walking around town. It was dark, and I'd be in my work clothes — we wore our own skirts and tops, and over that a black polyester apron with a bib. Not once, not twice, but three times, different policemen came up beside me to ask if I wanted a ride. I'd say, "No, I'm almost there!" [*laughs*] They probably thought I was crazy or at least needed protection.

I cried the first week I worked at the Blue Benn, but not because it was crazy busy.

My parents had the paint store, and I'd worked at all these shops downtown, and I think that back then, you just had to be "on" all the time. If a customer came in, and there were three customers behind them, you couldn't get nervous. You had to keep your cool. You had to be able to make change. You had to be able to think. You had to be able to say, "We're gonna be with you in a minute. We're making this; we're gonna do that."

Waitressing was very different, but I knew how to handle pressure. I did go home and cry, but what I cried over was different, probably, than what other people cried over. I was just blown away by how rude some people could be. I was a kid, I didn't know much about people who had absolutely no manners. I felt like saying, "You know I'm gonna bring you more coffee. You don't have to stick your cup out and point to it, I'm coming. That's my job." It took getting used to.

Working at the Blue Benn was exhausting. I only worked there for like a year and I gotta say, it was the most work I ever did. And I did a lot of work. It was just nonstop, and there were so many personalities, so many.

Mary Lou's a hoot, but geez, don't ever get her mad. Don't get Mary Lou mad. And I didn't. I did not get her mad. She had to be the hard-nosed one — almost like Sonny was a grown-up kid. I know that sounds terrible, because he wasn't; but he was. He's always trying new recipes; he was like every week — "Oh, try this!" Why? You've got 72 kinds of dressings! We only need tahini, that's all people ever ask for. I didn't even know what tahini was!

Sonny was just — just like his name. He was just a ray of sunshine. He was always happy, he always wanted to learn — he really had a love for cooking and trying things. And that, I thought, was so neat. He was very youthful. He really, really liked going places and seeing new things, and for someone who — I mean, he was probably in his 50s, maybe even early 60s by then, and I just thought it was so interesting, so cool. He was super sensitive, he would dress up, he was wicked into his hair, he would dye his hair, he was always tan, he would wear chains, like gold chains — but then again, Mary Lou, she had her ears pierced up to here [points to the curvature in her upper her ear], and they were always changed to

Neon sign details, circa 1970s

Pat Shepard, right, "was the best waitress I've ever known. It was like you were coming into her home. ... Her demeanor, the way she moved, it was all about making you comfortable, and her being the best that she could be."

—Eileen Main

the month of the birthstone month, graduating how big the stones were. [*laughs*] What a great couple. Sonny was such a lovely man, and he loved Mary Lou. I mean, he *loved* Mary Lou.

I know it sounds ridiculous, but I loved the waitresses that I worked with. I loved them. ... I actually worked with Frieda, who just passed away. I'm actually going to Frieda's house tonight to help her daughter clean out some of her stuff. She was a good friend to me when I was there.

And then there was Pat. Oh my god. She was the best waitress I've ever known. It was like you were coming into her home. That's what it was like. And when she waited on you, it was like you were at her dining room table — I mean the way she even just would wipe down the table. It was amazing. Her demeanor, the way she moved, it was all about making you comfortable, and her being the best that she could be. She was always like that. She was incredible.

She was very kind, but yet, even though she was kind, she could be very honest. She was one of the few people that would tell me, "OK, you cannot do" whatever and that was so helpful.

After a year, I didn't know what I wanted to do, but I knew I needed to get out of Bennington. I needed to know I could go someplace else. Of course by then I had fallen in love with my husband, who was 10 years older than me. ... [*laughs*] We met at my parents' store. He had just gone to wallpaper school and he came in to the store. He'd come into the Blue Benn and flirt with me, play my favorite songs on the jukebox and — that was kinda cute.

I ended up going to Washington, D.C., staying with my cousin. I only stayed there for eight weeks. I missed Jim. I missed my boyfriend, and I missed my family and I missed Bennington. Even though I was in the big city, I was very ... well, I was a country kid. I wrote postcards to the Blue Benn waitresses, and then Mary Lou said I could come back.

If one memory sticks out it was working at the Benn when we had that horrible storm in October 1987. I didn't work the first day; I worked the second day, and I just remember, the only place that had power was McDonalds and us. I remember that the people that came in just looked so tired and sad and wiped out.

Mary Lou worked those days — now, she didn't always — she wasn't really a waitress at that point. She would just come in and get important things done. And I remember she was there, and Sonny was there, and the cooks were there, and extra people were around. We fed as many people as we could. The customers paid; it wasn't like it was free, but it was just a different feeling, as if we were there to take care of people.

Mary Lou and Sonny were like, "We have to do this. We have to be open, because people are hungry, and they need us." I remember, when we finally closed, they fed us as well. We all sat down, and Mary Lou said, "Order something to eat, because I want everyone to eat before they go home." They wanted to make sure we didn't go hungry. I think they probably figured that a lot of us wouldn't have electricity when we got home.

Those two did a lot of sweet things. Oh, god, thinking back is funny. I had fun there. I did. I had fun and I definitely learned a lot about people. I grew up there.

Pat Shepard

A steep trail cuts through the woods over the Monroe property and levels off into fields and farmland, unfolding over miles. For Sonny and his little sister Pat, the deep woods were their magical playground, ending where the trees and meadows met. Sonny loved to push the limits of that childhood boundary, adventuring to farms and far-off swimming holes, always coaxing Pat to join him. Their three-year age gap never mattered to them as kids. "Sonny and I always got along," says Pat, looking back nearly 70 years. "We spent most of our time outside … and we were always together." As she grew up, her big brother looked out for her in different ways, eventually hiring her at his diner where she worked for 37 years — one of the Blue Benn's most beloved waitresses.

I'm 76, widowed with three children — two boys and a girl. Sonny's my brother.

I remember us growing up in North Bennington, where Mary Lou lives now. My dad owned all that land. I don't know what the acreage was, to be honest, but it seemed like a lot to us. Dad gave the land to Sonny and Mary Lou for them to build on.

We used to cross the road and climb the hill into the woods. We'd go up there every day or, in the winter, down to the pond in front of the property to skate. We always did things together. We have a brother, Gary, who's six years younger than me, so he was nine years younger than Sonny. That's a big gap for kids. It was like we didn't really know him, you know what I mean? He was just so much younger that we were. Kids are like that.

The Levers, the Tobins — we're all relatives, cousins — they lived nearby. We'd all stick together and do fun things — kid adventures. We spent most of our time outside, not like kids nowadays that want to stay inside, playing those Nintendo games — [*laughs*] I guess it's not Nintendo anymore. No, we were outdoors all the time.

By the time Sonny got his driving license, he was just a hell-ier. Oh my god. A lot of times he'd take me with him, but not always. You know what I mean? We'd drive

Above and opposite: Siblings, Pat and Sonny
Courtesy Pat Shepard

around; we'd have a bunch of kids with us, a bunch of teenagers. We made friends with a lot of the Bennington kids. As we got older, there were two carloads of us that used to drive to Guptill's down in Latham, near Albany. The roller skating rink. That's where Sonny met Mary Lou.

Sonny was a terrible tease. I remember when I was a teenager I had a boyfriend from Bennington. He'd get out of school and somebody would drive him over to North Bennington, where I went to school, so he could walk me home. Back then we used these zippered notebooks and we'd carry our books back and forth to school every day. So this boy is walking me home from school, and we get to the foot of my hill. I don't remember why, but he stops and opens my zippered notebook. Sonny, the wise guy, had put a pair of my clean underpants in there. The boy says, "Don't you have underpants on? Why is there a pair hidden in this?" I was so embarrassed. I tried to explain it had to have been my big brother who put them in there, but I probably couldn't even talk. Oh my god, I was embarrassed. [*laughs*]

He'd just come out with the funniest pranks. I'll never forget the day that Sonny told me to talk to his French teacher, Miss Tifft. I wasn't taking French then; you had to be in a higher grade. So Sonny said to me, "Go into Miss Tifft's class during break and say to her, "Voulez-vous coucher avec moi ce soir." Of course, I had no idea what I said. She was shocked, "Patty! Where did you get that from?!" She wouldn't even tell me what I said. I had to confess that my brother told me to ask her that. Sonny finally told me I'd asked her if she'd go to bed with me. The teacher really reamed him out for that. [*laughs*]

My dad was a woodworker and a superintendent at the Shea Products furniture mill in North Bennington. He had a workshop set up in the garage, and I remember the bandsaw. I'm pretty sure that he showed Sonny how to cut out chair seats on the bandsaw — that would have been his side job, before he got into cooking.

Daddy was a good woodworker. He built me a corner hutch and all the cupboards in my house. He was very creative. He could just look at a picture and build it. I loved working with my father. He would show you how to do something; he would train you to do it. He was a good teacher.

But for Sonny his creative side was all about cooking. The meals, that was his go-to. His first job was in the Vermont Restaurant, as a cook. That's when he really established his cooking.

I think that's where he got his big training. He had a mind for all these different dishes. I can remember this mushroom dish that he used to make. It was for breakfast. And it was like a French dish, because I can remember this one customer, René — he was a Frenchman — and he just loved that dish. He would come in on Sundays and get that dish. Oh, yes, he just loved that dish.

Sonny always looked out for me. When I was looking for a job after the mill closed, it was Sonny who told me they were they were looking for a waitress at the Vermont Restaurant and I got the job. I can remember him working there — it was a huge place with so many tables and they had great pizza and everything. There were two cooks, two waitresses in the daytime, a bartender and a barmaid. But what I remember most was that the waitresses called out the orders and Sonny would remember them. They'd call it out, and Sonny would have it. If you've ever worked in a kitchen, you'd understand that's amazing.

It was the same in the Blue Benn, but Sonny was the only cook that could do that. Any other cook, the waitress had to put a ticket down. When you stop and think: you've got three waitresses, hollering in the orders, sometimes at the same moment. That's hard, but Sonny was so good, he could handle it.

I got to the point, the past few years of working, I only worked Tuesday, Wednesday, Thursday. My husband got sick with Alzheimer's and Lisa and Mary Lou were so good about letting me arrange my schedule. Also, by then business was kind of slowing down, we closed at four. We had been open until eight o'clock Wednesday, Thursday and Friday nights, but they cut back the hours, because people just weren't coming anymore nights.

The past five years, Mary Lou was mostly taking care of Sonny. Who wanted to complain to Mary Lou about any problem in the diner? I couldn't do it. Lisa tried to be the boss, but she had enough to handle. She was trying to help her mother out with Sonny and run the diner. I think she did a good job, but she was so worried about her mom, her dad, and her mom taking care of her dad. It was an enormous distraction. I didn't want to give her any more problems.

The Blue Benn was always a happy place. It was sad that at the end there was so much distress in there. I was just shocked, the day it closed. I went in to work at ten-thirty, and I was told, "We're closing at two," and it was like, really? I was shocked. I just was so shocked.

I think Sonny made working at the Blue Benn easy for me. He really made me feel comfortable being a waitress. But the customers, I loved the customers. I really loved the customers. And that's what I miss right now. I watched so many kids grow up. They'd come in with their families when they were this big [*holding her hand knee-high*] and it was like, wow, I helped raise them. [*laughs*] I fed those kids their whole lives.

The only reason I'd go back would be for the customers, because I really did love my customers. But I'm 76 now and with the new owner, it's not gonna be the same. I'm just gonna see Sonny all around. ... I'll always feel him there. It's just — [*voice breaking*] now that it's sold, that part of Sonny is gone too.

Jim Woodward

Brian Carpenter

This interview with cook Brian Carpenter took place at the Blue Benn in 2001, when Carpenter had been on the job for three years. He continues in that role today. Carpenter was questioned by PhD candidate Marie-Pierre Huguet, with assistance from Sandy Sumner. (For more background, see the interview with the couple on page 97.)

Q: So, how long have you been working here?

A: Three years now.

Q: And this is the first place you worked in?

A: No, I've worked at the Northside Diner, and I started out at Geannelis' restaurant with Dick Geannelis. He was a great guy. Then I went on to the Northside Diner, I'm not sure what year it was, for a year, and then I went to the Paradise, where I worked for 15 years, maybe 16.

Q: How does it compare to the other places?

A: It's fast, like when I was at Geannelis', but when I was at the Paradise it was more laid back, you know. There I made roast beef, seafood, and here it's pretty much the same food, but it's just faster.

Q: How do you manage that?

A: That's hard.

Q: How many meals do you prepare at once?

A: At once? We can seat 40 people so by the time the order comes in … we got your food ready … so …

Q: So what, maybe seven?

A: No, no, 20 to 25 we can do at once.

Q: Wow.

A: Then that comes out and the other 25 come in and then you know. …

Q: What shift do you like best?

A: I like when I open in the morning because you're here by yourself.

Q: What time?

A: One o'clock. Yesterday I worked from 1:00 a.m. to 11:00 a.m. I only do that two days a week but last week I did it more because someone was hurt.

Q: So you do all the shifts?

A: Oh yeah, I do breakfast, lunch and dinner.

Q: Do you ever get the dishes mixed up? You have an amazing variety to keep track of.

A: Not really, but there are a few that would be very, very easy to get mixed up. Just now I did like seven people at a time, everything from your veggie meatloaf to your gyro (pointing at the interviewers' dishes) to a mac and cheese. … I mean, it's hard, but in the kitchen, it's all right there.

Q: Would you prefer a bigger kitchen or is this just right?

A: I'd prefer a little bigger because it is small.

Q: How many of you are there in there?

A: Not a lot. One, two, uh three guys at a time. One's a dishwasher, one or two are cooks. You can't put more than three guys in there. … I mean it's so small, and we're not big guys either.

Q: How do you deal with the heat, like in the summer? It must be at least 90 degrees in there.

A: Yes it is. On a really hot day I bet it is closer to 95, 100 or 105. I don't think it can be more than that.

Q: At the end of an eight-hour shift you're wiped out.

A: Not if you work eight hours. I usually work a 12-hour, you know.

Q: Now, when you work with the other cooks do you ever overlap dishes? Do you have specialties? How does it work?

A: Sometimes we do forget what the other guy's doing, like if he's got that going, and I do too, and I don't see it.

Q: What do you think of the vegetarian offerings?

A: I think they're great, really great. … We do a lot of Mexican food, too. Taco salads, fajita salads, we do a lot of wraps.

Q: I've noticed that in the morning each of you guys seem to work on a specific side of the kitchen.

A: Yeah, one guy takes one side and the other guy takes the other side. One of us looks at all the tickets and repeats what we gotta do. He makes eggs, toast, French toast, pancakes. The other guy does the omelets and mainly running around. … Breakfast is tough. People order pancakes and we only have one grill about the size of this table. Meanwhile, you're trying to grill pancakes for a group of five.

Q: Is the work satisfying? Do you feel like you've accomplished something at the end of the day?

A: All the time, yeah. All the time.

Q: You seem to like it.

A: I live for it.

Q: Right, it takes a special kind of skill.

A: Yeah, it does take that.

Q: And a good memory.

A: Yeah, good memory. I love it. I mean, I live for it.

Q: Did you go to school for this?

A: No, I just worked for a lot of people.

Q: You just picked it up?

A: That's right. I started when I was, I think, 13 years old, you know, and began to pick it up then. I learned a lot; I learned a lot with Sonny.

Q: Do you create some of the dishes?

A: I made up the stuffed eggplant with spinach and feta cheese. That was one of my creations, also the Cape Cod Deluxe. …

Q: When you come up with something, do you test it?

A: Sometimes we do, sometimes we don't. I always try one.

Q: On your days off do you come here to eat?

A: No, no. Actually, I only have one day off, and I have a little girl and I try to spend it with her. …

Q: You bet.

Jean Andrew

When Jean Andrew talks about veterans, her voice softens. Solemn and respectful, she describes them in a way only someone familiar with a soldier's life could. Her only son served six months in Iraq with the 101st Airborne, and braved two tours in Kosovo. "We loved our vets at the diner," she says warmly, recalling days when she and another waitress would pick up the tab of a returning soldier or Mary Lou's policy of offering deep discounts to service men and women on Veterans Day. With the Vermont Veterans' Home just across the road, Mary Lou and Sonny took honoring vets to heart. For them, Jean says, "It was just a part of how they took care of the community."

I'm 60 years old and have lived in Bennington — let me see, my son is 40; he's the oldest of three — so 40 years. My father always said I was on the head start program. [*laughs*]

I've been waiting tables since I was eighteen, so that's 42 years' experience under my belt. I worked at the Paradise Restaurant twice, under two different owners. I worked at the Mount Anthony Country Club. The second time I worked at the Paradise, business started getting really slow. It was probably around the year 2000. So I went to cash a paycheck at my bank, from the Paradise, which wasn't a very big check — you know, because of waitress pay — and it bounced. So I said, I gotta look for a different job.

I didn't hear if Mary Lou was hiring or not, but at

the time when I put an application in, there was a girl leaving — I was lucky because nobody ever leaves there. I got her position and that was in the end of May 2000. So I spent almost exactly 20 years working at the Blue Benn.

Not long after Jean started at the Blue Benn, she was featured in a Bennington Banner *article about the diner. "Andrew has worked for the Blue Benn for just over a year now, and she says with the fullest confidence that it's hands-down the best place to wait tables in the town of Bennington. Andrew said that statement at the tail end of an 11-hour shift, having just completed a workload that would drop the average human being."*

I remember that article. [*laughs*] … It was the best job, but it was also tough. It was different from what I was used to — working family-style restaurants, banquets, weddings. The Blue Benn was a very fast pace.

I did a lot of fill-in hours if somebody needed time off. I'd always be willing to go in and work. On average we'd work 10- or 11-hour shifts. You couldn't even count the number of tables, because there's three booths on each side, and ten stools on each side of the counter, and if you were third girl that night, you did a lot of the dishes and helped the other girls beverage their customers, or cleaned their tables and set up for them — and did cash; take the people's money and checks; cash them out.

It was hard work, but the family, Mary Lou and Lisa and Sonny, were all such hard workers, crazy-hard workers. I never worked for people that worked so hard. That was very admirable — they kinda set a standard that way. I've also never worked for more caring people in my life. They'd pay for your paid vacation, if you took a vacation, and they'd give you a Christmas bonus every year. They always paid us more waitress pay than you would get anywhere else.

And there were the little things. You know? One time something was wrong with my car and it was in the shop, so Sonny just took off from the diner to give me a ride to work. And Mary Lou, she is such a caring person. She even texted me this morning, because she remembered it was my father's birthday — Pearl Harbor Day. She remembers the kids' birthdays, the grandkids or whatever. After my father passed, Mary Lou had the cooks make a big meat platter for my family. She'd never forget your birthday. She'd never forget the day you started work — she'd write happy whatever-anniversary, on your time card, or Happy Birthday. They'd put up birthday signs for you, if you were working that day. Just kindnesses. That all made us, all the people that worked at the diner, feel incredibly loyal.

The Blue Benn's menu offered an eclectic assortment of dishes, but still managed to deliver on diner classics. Roadfood*, the landmark guide to cross-country American cuisine, endorsed the Blue Benn as "a true-blue hash house" where whole turkeys were roasted almost daily for hot turkey sandwiches and pies and donuts were made in-house in the cramped kitchen.*

What's the "pie story"?

[*Laughs*] Well, Mary Lou probably wouldn't want me to tell you this, but I have to tell you.

Sonny, he was a great cook, a great baker. He used to make the best donuts. Well one day, he made an apple pie, which looked just delicious. I was working my shift and he'd already left. I guess I had a customer who ordered a slice. So I tried to cut the first slice nice and straight,

Jean and her father, Gene Salluzzo, a U.S. Navy veteran

Lisa LaFlamme, Bridget Wysocki, and Pat Shepard. "I loved Elvis. We used to play 'Blue Christmas' around Christmastime ..."
— Jean Andrew

but it broke a little bit, the pie and the filling. I was never very good at cutting pie.

So the next morning I walk into the diner and above the dishwasher — we used to call that space the Wall of Shame. Our schedules were posted there and mistakes we'd made on a check or something, they'd highlight them to show us what we did wrong. Anyway right there on the Wall of Shame, Sonny'd put a sign up [*laughs*]: "Who the fuck took an ax to my apple pie?"

Sonny had a great sense of humor. He was funny and he was kind.

Sometimes, Jean says, it seemed like the staff offered its own brand of a comedy act to the customers. There was the time when customers got a full Laurel and Hardy routine thanks to a leaky pipe at the counter.

It was Bennington Battle Day, the day of the big parade, and it was on a Sunday, so of course the place was packed. The diner's sinks are underneath the counter, where we keep our cloths to wipe down or whatever. Sharon and I are out front and it's really busy. All of a sudden, water starts shooting out from the faucet. Everyone in the place could see the water spurting and we're like "Oh my god, what is going on!?" I tried to stop it with my thumb, but that didn't work. Meantime the customers are laughing and laughing. Brian [the cook] finally got it shut off from down below. It was pretty funny. A good show. [*laughs*]

Another time, Jean recalls, a man hoisted a high chair above his head as he worked his way back to his booth. The top of the chair accidentally hit a ceiling fan, causing a loud rat-tat-tat blast that sounded to Jean like gunfire.

So I got down like that, on the ground, because I got scared. Of course, everyone laughed, but I think they understood. It was shortly after 9/11. Scary times.

What do I miss the most? Everything. The customers, the job —I miss the kids. I used to love to see the kids and watch them grow up. A lot of times I'd give the kids a dollar or something, to play the jukebox. Everybody loved those jukeboxes.

When I'd get done with my shift on Monday — we always had to count the drawer and make a bank for the next day — I always would put some quarters in the jukebox and play my favorite songs while I was counting money. "Blue Velvet," by Bobby Vinton. I loved Elvis. We used to play "Blue Christmas" around Christmastime and Patsy Cline all the time.

And on Monday nights when I was alone and I'd lock the place up, I'd always say, "Goodbye, Blue Benn. Thanks for a nice day." It was kinda my tribute to the place.

Sharon Gavin

We hadn't been talking long when Sharon started to cry. "My parents died when I was in my early twenties. My mom when I was 21, and my dad when I was 23. That's pretty much around the time I started working for Sonny and Mary Lou. And those two," Sharon says, her voice taut. "If I ever needed anything, Mary Lou was always there. And Sonny, well he'd just crack me up. Always did." At 60, Sharon has worked at the Blue Benn for 33 years, one of the diner's longest-serving staff. In the end she says, it was just too hard for Mary Lou to tell the staff the diner had closed for good. "I don't think she could've done that, it was just too upsetting. We're all part of her family."

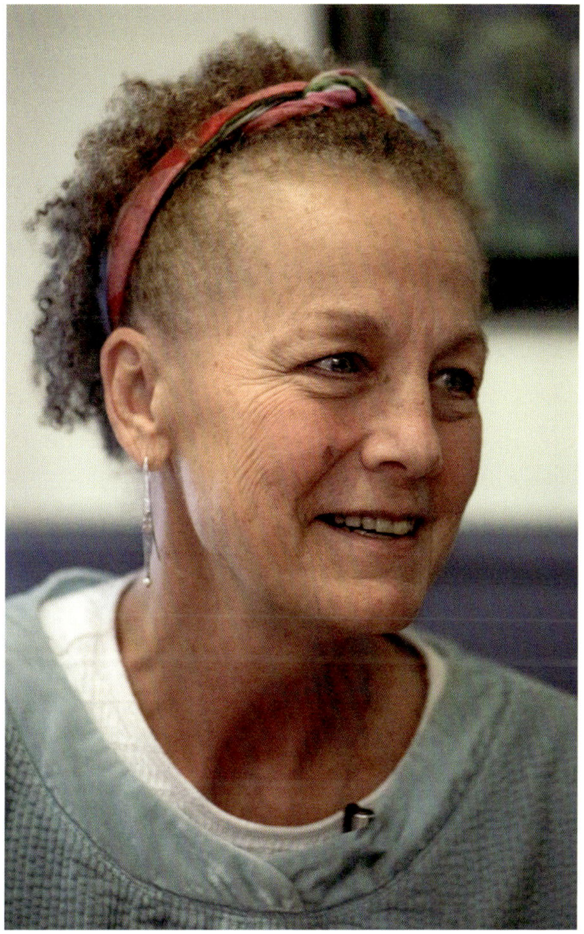

"I always believed serving people, making them feel better, was good work — meaningful work."
— Sharon Gavin

I graduated high school in '79. I was waitressing at another local breakfast spot when Mary Lou and Sonny — well, they kinda' poached me. [*laughs*] I started with 'em, I think it was about '82 or so. And I worked for about 12 or 13 years, then I went away for five years and did automotive bookkeeping work. But I came back to the diner, I think it was around '98.

It was always fun. Sonny – he was always very lighthearted. Back in the eighties we used to close on weekends at two in the afternoon. And we were all young. Most of us were all in our twenties and stuff when we started. We all liked to have our fun. And Sonny used to come back about three in the afternoon and ask, "Who wants to go have a drink?" [*laughs*] We'd go to the Vermont House over in Wilmington. They had front-porch seating out there, so we'd sit out on the porch and have a couple of beers. Sonny was always ready to go have some fun. [*laughs*]

With Mary Lou and Sonny, it was like the sign at the diner said, "I may be captain but my wife is the admiral." If something needed to be rectified, it was Mary

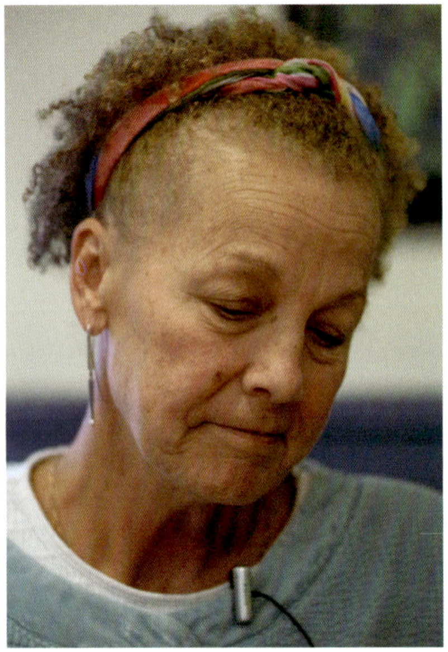

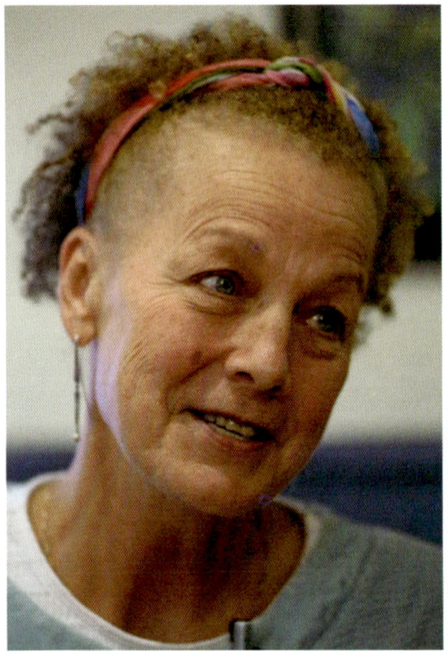

Lou in charge. "Sharon, go out in the back booth. Mary Lou wants to see you." You know? [*laughs*] She was the stern one. She would be the one that would give us our talkings-to and stuff like that. But, oh boy, she loved us. No doubt about that.

With Mary Lou, if you had a problem — well, she'd be crying with you too. Any time any of us had anything wrong, you say one word to her, "Oh, what can I do for you? Do you need help? Do you need anything?" She's been like a mom for me in my later years. It was easy to talk to her and stuff.

Sharon stops talking for a moment and holds up her hands, as if to bookend a moment in time. Sighing, she picks up the thread and continues, her hands curled tightly under chin.

You've gotta understand that Mary Lou had known my parents. We'd come into the diner in the sixties when I was a little kid. Of course, that was way before they owned it. Mom and Dad would bring us in and we'd sit at the counter. So working here, in a way, felt a little bit like coming home.

And working there, it was like family. We were like brothers and sisters. We'd be fighting one day and you'd have to apologize 'cause you can't leave mad 'cause you have to see each other the next day. You know? But through it all, I always looked forward to coming to work. For me it really was a second home. And I've been here a long, long time. When I started, you could smoke out front. Us girls had our ashtrays on the counter. Take a puff, go wait on somebody. Can you imagine? Smoking while we were working! It wasn't any big ordeal back then. [*laughs*]

The best part of working there? It was the customers. We were all willing to have fun with our customers and they loved it. And you'd always ask families how everybody's doing. And that's one thing good about seeing the same people year after year. I mean, we waited on babies and now they're in their twenties and they're bringing their babies in.

But we've lost a lot of customers through the years too. Mostly 'cause of bad times. It used to be different – back in the eighties and the nineties when it was good and money was good — at six in the morning our counters would be full with the carpenters, the painters, the town workers. And you'd see them every other day or every day sometimes, even if it was just coffee or donuts. But you knew what they were gonna have so they'd come in, you'd throw a coffee down at 'em and say, "Usual?" "Yeah, all right." And it was full. And nowadays your construction workers can't afford to come in and eat every day. Those were the good days.

And we had all the Bennington College kids back then too. Oh, they were fun back in the eighties. They were the funkiest people. They'd always dress outrageous — the Goodwill stores and stuff. And you knew they had a good night the night before, you know? We always could set our watches by it. By about noon, maybe one o'clock they'd start comin' around the corner. It was like, "Well, all right, they slept until noon. They got up, had another beer, or they smoked a joint and they're on their way in."

They ate a lot. But a lot of 'em were vegetarians and Bennington College didn't do vegetarian food back then. So Sonny figured that out and put vegetarian options on the menu. I can't always tell the Bennington College kids anymore 'cause they're kinda more … I don't know, normal? A few of 'em you can. But not like it used to be. They were always so fun. They would talk to you. "Hey, what's going on?" Ask you stuff about your life. They were just good kids.

I remember one girl, she'd gone to school at Bennington for four years and her parents had come down every once in a while and visit with her. They were always very nice to us and we enjoyed 'em. And we'd want 'em to have a good time. I can get casual with people, you know? [*laughs*] So, I'd just served him breakfast one day and he's, like, "I'll have my donuts to go." So I gave him his donuts and the check and he puts the check down with the money under it. We were busy and they left. And I went to pick up the check and there was an extra $100 bill sitting there. I'm, like, "Oh, wait. I gotta go out and find him. He left me too much!" [*laughs*] So I ran outside and I'm, like, "Sir, you've left too much." And he's, like, "No. That's for your service to our family over the years." That was nice.

Once in a while we'd get a bad customer. One guy — he was very rude — Mary Lou actually kicked him out. He made some sexual comments and stuff and we'd known him for quite some time. Mary Lou came over and said, "That's it, that's the last straw. There's no place for that in my diner," and she asked him to leave. That's one thing Mary Lou always held true: "If someone doesn't treat you with respect and you're respecting them, you have my permission to tell 'em to get up and leave."

We heard talk that the kitchen was once or twice used as an emergency room. Any comments on that?

One of my doctors, a regular. … Now, he's pretty close to retirement and I don't want to get him in trouble, but he was just great. He stitched me up in the kitchen. [See the interview with Jeff Yucht on page 131 for the doctor's version of the story.]

I just was cleaning out our dish drain back in the kitchen and there was a piece of glass in there that I didn't spot. Suddenly, I've slit my thumb open. Luckily, this doctor was out front. I had it all wrapped up and stuff and I had a glove on, but it was bleeding through. He's like, "Gee, Sharon, what'd you do?" And there I am trying to serve him lunch. I say, "I cut it. [*whispering*] Can you stitch me up?" And he's, like [*whispering*], "Let me run to the hospital and get some equipment first."

So he took off and he comes back down a little while later and — I don't know if we should say this — 'cause we were out by the back door on the cutting table by the kitchen door and he's stitching up my thumb. It took about five minutes. I only had three stitches. So that was all right. I gave him a free lunch.

Good times and bad times, we've all had 'em. And our customers, the same thing with them. We go through it with them. Some lose children we've served since they were babies. You lose 'em at an early age and that's devastating for all of us. 'Cause … we're all part of this community and we feel it.

After all these years, are you glad to move on?

No. I mean, I'm 60 now and it's tough work. I mean, there are times when you're waiting on 24 people at once, but we all have a rhythm. We all have our ways of doing things. And that's a good thing. I always believed serving people, making them feel better, was good work — meaningful work.

Sharon, left, with co-workers, early 1980s

Handshakes all around after the game.

Six-year-old Emily Shaw

Vermont Living

section 3

The Sunday Rutland Herald and the Sunday Times Argus, June 12, 1983

Photos by Vyto Starinskas

Blue Benn customers bite into hamburgers, or are they nut-burgers?

Chowing Down At The Blue Benn

By PAUL TEETOR

It started out as a simple recipe in a health-food magazine, a great substitute for a hamburger — a nut-burger,

chopped onions and Monroe's secret tahini dressing.

Monroe developed his following the old-fashioned way: He earned it.

The lunch-time waiting line for

eating huevos rancheros — Mexican-style eggs;

— A woman factory worker who eats Monroe's fried or broiled fresh seafood three or four times a week;

— A local drug counselor eating

Rutland Herald and Times Argus, June 12, 1983

CHAPTER FIVE

CUSTOMERS

HERSHEY'S
SYRUP

Normand LeBlanc

The Breakfast Club

If Norm LeBlanc were cast as a movie character, he would play Radar O'Reilly in M.A.S.H. Not because of his looks — physically he's the polar opposite of the pocket-sized sergeant — but because of his unique ability to procure surplus stuff discarded or forgotten by the U.S. military. After four years in active duty and 20 years as Naval reservist, retiring as a senior chief petty officer, Norm knows "the ins and outs of the government surplus system." It's been a boon for North Bennington, where by his own estimates the village has acquired well over a million dollars' worth of equipment at bargain-basement prices. Since 2008, Norm has been the highway superintendent there. His love affair with Sonny's Blue Benn began in the 1990s, shortly after leaving active duty. The diner quickly became part of his daily routine: "I'd say, for the last ten years, I never even had to order. I'd just walk in."

I guess you could say that I'm always trying to put the right thing in the right place, for the right person. Having been in the military, where everybody wants to say No changed me. "No" is easy; say "Yes." Help someone succeed. Never walk by a mistake. Fix it.

I was born in New York state and moved here on my first-year birthday. I'm 51 years old. I grew up in Wood-

ford. My parents owned the Peter Pan Motel. My father had gone overseas, the Korean War, and came home — he was a Seabee, my grandfather was a Seabee and I'm a Seabee [U.S. Naval Construction Battalion].

It's funny, in my 24 years in the Navy I was on an Army ship for three days, sailing from Kuwait to Bahrain, and that's the only sea time I've ever had. What the Navy Seabees do is build piers, boats, hospitals, schools. I worked on construction vehicles: trucks, bulldozers, backhoes.

I started going to the Blue Benn when I first got out of the service. I went there every day and sometimes twice on Fridays. I'd take my wife out to dinner there, when our kids were somewhere else. She liked their pancakes. My favorite was probably biscuits and gravy. They'd serve that on Tuesday.

I think my favorite day was Thursday. You see more of the early-morning regulars on Thursdays. It was more of a bonding day. There was Kathy Kennedy Kenyon — she was a teacher — and there was Albert Krawczyk — he was an everyday guy. There was a whole group of us. There was Frank, who was retired, and Alan an electrician and the pharmacist and Brian, the afternoon dispatcher for the police department. And there was the oatmeal guy [Willard Boepple]. He used to try to get me to eat healthier. Me and Willard are friends, even though we are the odd couple. In fact people can't believe that somebody like me would hang out with a guy like him. We still have lunch together.

In the last four or five years, there was another fella. He had a Philly omelet every day. That's exactly what he had. And on Thursdays, the Green Mountain Power guys would also come in.

And for a while this fella named Don Goodrich came in. He'd sit at the far end. I never got a chance to really talk to Don but twice in my life. He was a lawyer by trade, and his son died in the World Trade Center on 9/11. Don had actually been to Afghanistan to help children there. He was a really cool guy, but he kept to himself. I really wish I could've talked to him, just because of my own experiences.*

The diner attracted people from different backgrounds, different walks of life. There were plenty of mornings when we'd have some heated political talks on all kinds of subjects, but everybody respected each other. Usually Lisa would squash the big argument, because they would be on Friday, when the diner was a little more full, and she'd say, "That's enough. That's enough. Let's move along."

I always went for breakfast. I was there at six o'clock, four or five-thirty if they let me in. When we would be hauling snow from the town of Bennington, I would come over and help them sometimes, or if we were plowing on a snowy night I'd wheel in there at three-thirty in the morning, walk through the back door, and get my breakfast sandwich.

Sometimes I would just stop by. Brian always got there early to get his kitchen going and get everything ready for the day. I'd see the lights on, and I'd pull in, and go around back and kick the door a couple times. They were robbed once — Brian scared the guy off — and I didn't want him coming out with a rolling pin ready to hit me. I'd go in and ask him make me a breakfast sandwich.

For me the Blue Benn was family. We actually cared what went on in each other's lives. Probably my favorite story happened the day my father died. It was just a sad day. My father was in the vets home [across the street]. It was four o'clock in the morning, and that was the end of it. By the time we got through the process there, it was five-thirty, and I walked over to the Benn and Pat opened the door — besides Lisa, Pat was probably my favorite waitress. I sat there, and I actually cried and Pat was with me. After a bit I got up and walked out through the kitchen, and I couldn't even finish my breakfast.

You know, we were all family there. I've been over to Mary Lou's house; I've done work for them. I've had to go over one day to pick Sonny up after a fall, for Mary Lou. I helped Brian in the kitchen, every morning for 10 years, open his back window, because it'd take two people to open it, because he had to lean over all the stuff. It was — we were family, you know what I mean?

Well, probably my best memory is in 2001. As a reservist I was activated right after the towers fell. I got called at three in the morning. I was at the Blue Benn for breakfast by six and on a plane to Guam by noon. The next time I got activated, in 2004, I actually had some notice. We probably had four months' notice. So I left, actually, on Valentine's Day to go overseas — first to Mississippi and then Kuwait, Bahrain, Afghanistan. A friend of mine, Tom — who used to go to the diner quite a bit — arranged for the Blue Benn to be open at two in the morning, because I had to get to the airport that early. And it was a shock to me, because he picked me up, and he said, "Let's go down and get a cup of coffee." I figured we were just going to Stewarts or something. Well, we pulled into the Blue Benn, and that place was wall-to-wall people. And Lisa and Brian opened up, and the power guys were there ... all my friends — it was wall-to-wall.

When I got to Afghanistan, I sent that flag home that was flown on our base, and sent it back to the Benn. After that, I'm gonna say for the next eight years, I never bought my Thursday breakfasts. Sonny always paid for it.

Will it ever be the same again? I don't know. I've saved a fortune since it closed. I've put money away, $1,300 this year, just from not eating at the Blue Benn. What will I miss most? I'm a simple kind of guy. I loved the ambience of the place. It just felt like you belonged.

* *Editorial Note: Sarah and Donald Goodrich lost their 33-year-old son Peter, on Sept. 11, 2001. He was aboard the second plane to hit the World Trade Center. Struggling three years later with how to memorialize him with the $49,000 donated to them from family and friends, the couple helped start a school for girls in Afghanistan, supported by the Peter M. Goodrich Memorial Foundation. Sarah died of cancer in 2010. The foundation's work continues.*

Top: The counter nameplate where Normand sits. The Latin "ne radicem" tranlates to "grow no roots."

Above: Lisa LaFlamme and Brian Carpenter with a flag and proclamation Normand sent home from Afghanistan.

Opposite: On the job with the village Highway Department.

Willard Boepple

The Breakfast Club

Willard Boepple will not be contained. Thrilled to be back in his cavernous studio — a broken wrist landed him in hospital for weeks — he bounces from one idea to the next, energized by the thought of getting back to work. Lately he's been creating monoprints, layering shapes and overlapping colors to form intriguing new patterns and hues. The artist looks over at one of his abstract sculptures, a large construction that evokes a sense of architecture stripped to its barest bones. Until the pandemic, he says, his days began like clockwork with breakfast at the Blue Benn Diner. "It was my wakeup call," he adds, observing that those 6:00 a.m. starts were more than food with friends. "They were a border to my day."

Since I live and work in the same building, I find the line between work and home can get a little sloppy. You're not going to work, because you're already there. [*laughs*] The phone rings, and there's the book you're reading, distractions are everywhere. That border between work and home and leisure isn't clear. So the way I've dealt with that, and I have done for a long time, is to get up at six and go out for breakfast, go away for breakfast, and then come back to work. [*laughs*] I get home and I'm ready — the day starts.

I'm a sculptor and a printmaker. I was born in Bennington; I'm very local, in that sense. Grew up — did a lot of growing up out west, in California, from my teen years and into college; then back to New York, to study art at City College of the City University of New York and, later, at RISD [Rhode Island School of Design]. I taught briefly at Bennington College and for quite a while at the Boston Museum School.

My father was still living here in Bennington, so I came up a lot. One summer, just out of the blue, the sculptor Isaac Witkin asked me if I would work for him for the summer. He needed help. I realized, almost overnight, sculpture was where I belonged.

I really started going to the Blue Benn in the seventies, but not a lot, and I don't remember the first time. I

Willard Boepple's "Hourglass" monoprint, 2020

The Breakfast Club
Courtesy Kathy Kenyon

didn't eat out much back then except tablecloth dinners when I could afford it. I ate at home. Cooked at home. No, my real days at the Blue Benn began more recently, the nineties, and particularly breakfast.

As it happened, what I fell into was the six o'clock gang — the guys who were there at six, on their way to work: the electric guys, the road crew, George Elwell and what ended up as my crew. You end up sitting, habitually, in the same spot. There's your seat, your stool at the bar.

So you come in the diner, and the counter separates. That's where you enter into the kitchen. So to the right at the counter, George Elwell took the corner seat, and then Brent Peacock was the next guy in. Then I was usually next, and then Norm [LeBlanc] was on my other side. And then the Central Vermont guys were kind of down there, and Kathy [Kenyon] and the insurance people and, I didn't know them, were down the other end.

Of course, that was all part of the routine. You'd be there at six, and the door cracks open and the waitress leans out and the first thing that happens, before you get in, is the ashtray can gets bumpty-bumped down the step and is put out there. Then the door is flung open and she says, "OK, boys." [*laughs*] I'd often be first. Sometimes it was George or Norm. Anyway, then the coffee's on the counter by the time you sit, and in my case, the oatmeal would be there very shortly thereafter. [*laughs*] We never had to order, they just brought the food.

I'm the oatmeal guy. Famous for it. [*laughs*] Oatmeal, and then usually an egg, poached or scrambled, toast and coffee. Norm used to hammer me about the oatmeal. At the same time, he'd have the breakfast sandwich — you know, a slab of ham, eggs, a ton of mayonnaise if it wasn't hollandaise. This big, juicy thing. Norm's no slim chicken, and we used to give him a hard time about his heart condition. So I'd push the oatmeal near him and, just as he's sitting down, say to Lisa, "Lisa, we'll have double oatmeal today." Never worked. [*laughs*]

"Sonny would poke his head out now and again, but Mary Lou ran the show."

One of the great things about the Blue Benn was, of course, the atmosphere. It was unassuming and nobody got special treatment. You waited for a booth. Just because you were a really old hand didn't mean you swanned in and got a booth ahead of everyone else. No, sir.

The service was — well, the waitresses were all really pros. People grumble about some of them — [*laughs*] there's always grumbling, gossip, and the girls sort of squabbling amongst themselves, but they were pros.

By the time I was going regularly, Mary Lou wasn't there much in the morning at all. She would be working lunch and dinner. Whenever we overlapped, she was always warm. Clearly, she was up to speed — who's in, who's out, who's regular, who isn't. Sonny would poke his head out now and again, but Mary Lou ran the show. And what a job she did. She was such a presence. She was special. By the nineties, Lisa was in charge. But everybody described Mary Lou as the puppet master. [*laughs*]

People did talk politics in the Benn, but they were polite, mostly. I mean, it was civil. People would steer away from anything too sensitive. Norm and I, I mean, he used to say he liked talking to me because I would listen. [*laughs*] He'd say, "You're one of the few people I can totally disagree with, and still get along with."

Norm and I were on opposite sides of the Trump issue and much that preceded it. But I have a deep admiration for him and his military service and a lot of what he stood for. And where we overlapped were some wonderful places on the political spectrum, one of them being, we both believe in national service — that everybody 18 to 21 do a year or two of some kind of national service to create a connection between the young and their government, their country.

I wanted to make sure and tell you this: It might've been coolish outside, and people probably thought that it was warm in the Benn, because it was pretty crowded. Norm came in, and he was a little late, and he took off his jacket and he said, "Now, this is the American dream." And the smell of coffee, and the waitresses waiting to serve, to bring him his killer sandwich, and everybody there scootching over to make room for his spot, and the hum of conversation. It was just the way he said, "This — is the American dream," coming from this great big G.I. [*laughs*] It really stuck. I felt like I had my finger on the pulse of my community.

Collage by Kathy Kenyon

John & Kathy Kenyon

The Breakfast Club

John Kenyon's sisters always knew there was something special about Kathy. "My older sisters used to tease me about her when I was seven years old," says John. "They knew she was cute, and that I always liked her, but I was very shy." Their hunch that one day Kathy would steal John's heart was dead on, it just took longer than anyone expected. Fifty years to be exact. Both families were "thrilled" when the two finally did tie the knot, smiling at the notion that two of Bennington's biggest families — Kathy grew up with nine siblings and John twelve — were joining the clans together. Both Blue Benn fans from way back, the married couple would together create a new tradition: breakfasting at the diner every weekday on their way to work until John retired in 2012.

Kathy: We're both 69. John and I are both from North Bennington, born and raised. We were born two weeks apart, so we went through school, kindergarten through twelfth grade, together.

John: We've known each other our whole lives.

Kathy: North Bennington was a very small town. His family has 13 kids, and my family has 10. I'm number 6 in my family.

John: And I'm number 5 in mine. There's nine girls and one boy in Kathy's family, and there's eleven girls and just two boys in my family — so twenty gals and three boys in the two families combined.

Kathy: We pretty much filled the North Bennington grade school.

I always liked John, but back then there was no romantic interest in the least. Skip way down the road a bit for that. [*laughs*]

John: Ouch. [*laughs*]

Kathy: I always thought he was funny. He's a funny guy. But that was about it. And then — I don't remember

Normand LeBlanc behind the counter
Kathy Kenyon

what year it was — anyway, I was having my hair done by his sister, who used to own — and still does — a hair salon in Bennington. And she said, "You know, my brother is going through a divorce." I said, "Really?" I had divorced at that point. We were both about 50.

John: Fifty-one. [*laughs*] I believe it was the late summer of 2002.

Kathy: All right. So his sister said to me, "Boy, I wish I could find somebody that would treat me like John treated his wife." And of course, that stuck in my head. I'd been through a divorce — actually, I married the same guy twice and had two boys. So then his sister was talking to John — Linda, his sister — and said …

John: "Guess who [*laughs*] I just spoke to? And she is single."

We dated several years and got married in 2008. On our first date I actually snubbed the Blue Benn. When Kathy finally accepted our first date, she said to me "coffee only." Now, I used to go to the diner quite a lot with my previous wife, and of course, by myself, so the diner was pretty familiar to me. But when Kathy agreed to go out, I picked her up, and I drove her to Manchester, 30 miles away. I thought to myself, "I'm not gonna go around the corner to the Blue Benn Diner. Our date's gonna be over too soon."

Kathy: But we still became regulars at the Benn. It started out with the two of us going to the Blue Benn for breakfast and then to our respective jobs. We'd go every morning.

John: They were open at 6:00 a.m. so it was a convenient place for us to have breakfast together. At that time, I sold roofing materials in three states, so I was on the road a lot. I would usually start with Kathy at the diner. At 6:00 a.m. we'd be there and so would Norm [LeBlanc]. We'd be the first to arrive. The early start was convenient and the food was always great.

Kathy: And then I retired [as a teacher], and he continued working. By then I would go three days a week, mainly because Lisa [Monroe] was there. We'd developed a friendship. I told her just the other day, nobody butters my toast like you do. [*laughs*]

I used to eat in a booth with John, but when I started going on my own, when he was working, the regulars — our group — would all eat at the counter. I would walk in, and everybody would say hello, and we'd sit in our respective places up at the counter. We just cross-talked and laughed and … if somebody, a stranger, happened to be there and sat in your seat, eyebrows would be raised. [*laughs*] It really was like something out of *Cheers*. When it was over, I mourned losing the comradeship. To be honest, for me going to the Blue Benn was all about the social event. [*laughs*]

John: One scrambled egg, and she wouldn't eat the whole thing. If they could serve a half an egg, Kathy would ask for it, because she eats like a little bird.

Kathy: Actually, one of my favorite meals would be a piece of pie that Brian made.

John: Occasionally, you would have that for breakfast.

Kathy: Coconut custard pie — yeah, I would have that for breakfast.

John: For me, I would say an omelet. Probably the steak omelet — the Philly cheese omelet. That was one of my favorites. But there were so many favorites. We'd mix it up all the time. French toast, pancakes, poached eggs — they did a great job.

One thing I always admired about Sonny and Mary Lou was that they were very visible and approachable, and I think that added to their success. The diner was quite different from what it was when I first got to know it. I was 19 years old and in school. I went to work for Dick Manning, who at the time owned the Heritage House and the Blue Benn Diner. I was a cook at the Blue Benn, what you would call a grill cook; hamburgers, hot dogs, made sandwiches, French fries. I remember, at the time, Sonny worked at the Vermonter restaurant, around the corner and up the street.

"We became part of an unusual family — one of the regulars."

But back in 1970, there was only one highway that went north and south, so everybody who traveled Route 7 had to go by both [the Blue Benn Diner and the Heritage House], and Dick Manning capitalized on that. Back then you cooked right at the counter. I believe there was a small addition on the back that maybe the dishes were done in and a little bit of prep work, but you actually worked the grill and the Fryolator right there — everybody at the counter could watch everything you did.

But, here's the biggest thing … everything Manning did was based on the idea of portion control. He would actually kick you in the hind end if you made a sandwich with four-and-a half ounces, not four ounces. Every single thing — hamburger, all your sandwich meats, everything — was weighed. That's how he really controlled things. Sonny went completely the opposite direction. When you look at the diner's menu and the amount of food at the diner, it's a completely different perspective.

Kathy: The waitresses were also a big part of Sonny's Blue Benn. …

John: The sass. We encouraged the sass. [*laughs*] Heidi and Sharon. They could be quick with their tongue, but we always appreciated it.

Kathy: Once we learned that's what they were about. [*laughs*]

John: We enjoyed it. I remember one time I came in with two of my sisters and one of the waitresses came up to me and said so everyone could hear, "Wow. You sure know when the Kenyons are here." [*laughs*]

Kathy: Well, they're talkers and they're loud.

John: We became part of an unusual family — one of the regulars. We actually made acquaintances of people we never knew lived in the community. The more you'd see each other, the more you'd learn about what they did for work and the kind of personalities they had. We knew, and the waitresses knew, which customers you could tease and which ones you might not want to tease.

I would just say this — [Sorry, honey, *he says to Kathy, apologizing for interrupting*]: I think there was a recognizable intimacy at the Blue Benn Diner, with both the staff and the people who — the regulars who ate there. I mean, in the old diner — before Covid, that is — you hugged people.

Kathy: I looked at it as almost a second home. I really did. I developed friendships. It was a wonderful way to start my day, three days a week. It was just a warm place to be.

Lisa Monroe

Rutland Herald and Times Argus, June 12, 1983

Lynn Frost

Neighbors

The Tuscan Sunflower's golden-yellow door opens to a burst of green and the heady scent of roses. We sit near the floral cooler where buckets of fresh-cut flowers from pale pink to ice blue blossom behind glass doors. Lynn Frost bought her shop next door to the Blue Benn Diner three years ago, after 11 years there as Sonny and Mary Lou Monroe's tenant. "I had worked for another flower shop in town for more than 28 years and finally decided it was time to start out on my own." Lynn says, leaning forward to tell her story. "Not long after I made the decision, a woman who had a flower shop in Cambridge, New York, sent me a card. Now I'm not a packrat, but certain things I do hold on to." The card offered some simple advice: "Leap! And the net will appear." She did, and hasn't looked back since.

I'm 62 years old. I came to Bennington in 1978. I was newly married and my husband, Bill, had grown up here. I moved here to be with him. When I decided to go out on my own, I started looking around Bennington for a place to open a florist shop.

I'd see Mary Lou and Sonny if we went into the diner, but I didn't know them personally. You know, those were the owners of the diner kind of thing. So when we met them, it was interesting. We met upstairs in the apartment, which was Mary Lou's mother's apartment. Her mother had died years before, but the apartment looked just like the day her mother passed away.

We sat in this apartment, in the living room, and talked about me wanting to rent the space below that had always been a hair salon. Mary Lou was like, what do you want to do in here? So I told her. I still have a letter that she wrote to me after she met me for the first time. She said she could tell by talking to me and my husband that we were going to be successful and that we would make it work.

We rented the place and did a lot of renovations, because, like I said, it was a hair salon. We did things like the counters are made of trees from our property that my husband cut and we had them milled. And we ordered the cooler, and it came in pieces, and my sister and her husband came down and helped us build it and put it together. I mean it was a true family effort.

Once we finally moved in, I worked a lot of hours, crazy hours. There were times I'd be there, like before a holiday, really early in the morning, and Sonny would pop in, because of course he'd also be there before dawn. He'd just pop in the backroom and ask, "How's it going?" He was just — just kind of checking in on me. It was sweet.

The whole time we were renovating, we'd eat at the Benn a lot. The waitress always knew what we liked. My husband always ate the same thing for breakfast: two eggs over easy, home fries, hash, and one piece of wheat toast. And it was so funny that nobody ever asked him his order. They just knew what he wanted. My favorite? The Garden Scramble. It was basically a loose unstructured omelet that was full of vegetables.

Top to bottom: Sharon Gavin, Brian Carpenter, David LaFlamme, and Mary Lou Monroe

I was always comfortable with Mary Lou and Sonny as landlords. I had never rented before so it was a lot for me to learn. But I think we had a great relationship. The business part — sure, but also, I think we became friends. And even now, the day Mary Lou sold the diner, she called me and she said, "I've just gotta tell you, it really, actually happened." She always said I was the best tenant she ever had.

Honestly, starting the business was like jumping off a cliff — quitting my job with two children, one in college. I look back and realize how brave, maybe foolish, it was to have jeopardized my family like that. You know, twenty-eight-and-a-half years is a long time, but I felt as if other people, people who didn't even know me, Mary Lou for one, felt confident that I was gonna be able to make this happen.

"Sonny was an amazing gardener."

I never really saw Mary Lou and Sonny much together. Initially, they both were there when they met us about renting the building, but then we'd mostly run into them on their own. Mary Lou would pop in, or he would, but it wasn't like we would see them together. In the winter he would go to Florida or different places. But she didn't like going. And she'd say, "No, I want to stay right here." He seemed to like to adventure a little bit more than she did.

Sonny was an amazing gardener. So he loved coming in and seeing the flowers and the plants and — that was really fun. Truth is, I didn't really know how good a gardener he was until he died and Mary Lou showed me a lot of pictures and I saw his gardens at the house.

Looking back, Lynn acknowledges that what might be her favorite experience with the diner staff was a catastrophe for the Blue Benn and her florist shop.

I was closing one night when I saw a fire truck over at Mary Lou's. Oh my god, I thought, figuring there was a fire in the kitchen. So I ran next door to make sure they were OK, and they were pumping water. And Brian [the head cook] said to me, "We've got water pouring into the cellar." I asked why and he said he had no idea. I ran back to my shop, down to my cellar and, oh my god, I thought I would die. It was like a swimming pool.

Well, we were there all night long. The fire department's pump stopped working and they couldn't help us. We got a hold of a septic company that came out. We had a very, very old furnace down in the shop cellar — I mean the thing was like a hundred years old. So our mission was to try and save the furnace. Meantime, they were trying to pump out the Blue Benn's cellar. I mean they had food stored down there. It was horrendous. They actually had to close.

It was a catastrophe for both of us, worse for the Benn because they had to close. But we developed a real wonderful camaraderie. I was grateful that we became really good friends, and with the staff too, because we were there so much. It was wonderful. We were always calling and checking on each other — I just remember Brian when he'd see my car he'd call out to me. And Brian's got that really loud voice — "I SEE YOU'RE THERE. HOW'S THE WATER IN THE CELLAR?" [*laughs*]

It went on for months. And then, when they reopened, I put out my sandwich sign and put balloons on it and

said, "The Blue Benn is back open!" Mary Lou called me, and she was like, "Thank you so much." I said, "Well, people have to know."

That experience really made me feel good, watching out for each other.

What has Lynn missed most about Sonny's Blue Benn? Her answer speaks to what made the diner a Bennington institution:

Most mornings during workdays, I walked with a girlfriend. We'd go early in the morning, before we'd start our days. If it was raining or maybe too cold, we'd go to the Blue Benn instead, for breakfast. And there always were certain folks that were there, every weekday morning. I probably couldn't tell you their names, but they'd greet us, and each other every morning. I knew one person worked at the bank. I knew somebody else ran a snowmobile shop up on Woodford Mountain. And somebody else was a sheriff. Somebody else was a very old farmer kind of gentleman. And I loved that. And some mornings, depending on the weather or what was going on, conversations would happen between people that wouldn't normally happen. There was something very lovely about it. I think I'll miss that most.

Opposite and above: Plantings and notecard by gardener Rose Carlsen
Rose Carlsen

WASSICK'S TIRE SERVICE
WASSICK'S TIRE SERVICE
Willard Mountain
SKI DESTRUCTOR
TIRE
WASSICK
SERVICE
2005
2006

Donny Wassick

Neighbors

Don Wassick, who's mostly known around town as Donny, went into the family trade at 25 years old, after college and a stint as a ski instructor. At 63 he's worked at Wassick Tire Service most of life, building a business that's become a Bennington landmark. His looks — more silver-haired TV actor than garage owner — and laid-back manner are hard to square with a job that requires catering to often harried, demanding customers. Centering him is his family, whose photos dot the walls behind the shop register. One picture stands out. Taken in Paris at the end World War II, Steve Wassick Sr. stands should-to-shoulder with his brother, ready to come home. He brought with him skills in tire repair, learned working in the field on a jumble of military vehicles. "I pride myself on my family," says Donny, father of two and grandfather of two. "They've made all the difference in my life."

My dad started the business in 1946. He was actually over on North Street, across from the Bank of Bennington. He was only there for one year and then moved down here. He was in a partnership that he pretty swiftly bought out. Wassick Tire has been here ever since. In fact, this summer is our 75th year.

We're a very community-oriented business. We've got

a great customer base. We've worked hard to build that. I started out with my older brother in 1983, but I bought him out a few years later. He pursued his art career. So it all worked out.

The original Blue Benn opened in 1948, and of course my dad was here a year prior to that. Even back then, it probably started then, people would drop their cars off and go have breakfast or lunch next door at the Blue Benn. They'd be eating and we'd be working on their vehicles. It's been that way ever since. We've really, really missed it since Covid hit and they've shut down. Everybody that comes through the door says, "I always go to the Blue Benn. Where am I gonna go now?"

My first memory of the Blue Benn was my father taking me there when I was young — eight, nine, ten whatever. I remember, going in the door, we'd go to the left and sit at the counter. And the cook would be cooking your breakfast right behind the counter. They didn't have the kitchen in the back then. The grill was right there. I remember watching them cook our meals right in front of us. I can still see the grill, and the grease flying when the hamburgers would go on, or the pancakes and bacon. [*laughs*] It was just pretty neat. For some reason, I just remember that so clearly.

The Benn, circa 1977
From "The Rock Ribs of Bennington Town"
Julie Snow

Of course Mary Lou and Sonny didn't buy the place until 1974. I was in high school. It's funny, I remember I had a free period in the morning so I'd drive over and have breakfast — bacon and eggs and hash browns. Actually I'd trade off between that and Eggs Benedict.

We'd go there as high school kids. We'd take over a couple of booths. Of course, they always had the jukeboxes so we'd come prepared with dimes to play music. It was a lot of fun — just kids goofing around. You'd always get the regulars in there, but they weren't bothered. It was a very friendly atmosphere.

When I started working here, I'd go more often. I go there more in the winter. I always like to run over and get some hot soup or a grilled cheese sandwich, what have you. But my family loves to go there. My kids, my grandkids, we all do. My grandkids are always really interested in the jukeboxes. Just like we were when we were kids. [*laughs*]

I can't say the family had a set routine, but we did like to go there on Sunday mornings. Of course, it'd be extremely busy; we'd have to wait in line. And in the later years, even if we had to run up for an early lunch, we'd still have to wait in line. It got so popular.

A lot of stuff would happen in the waiting room, a lot of conversations. There'd always be somebody from out of state or from out of town, and I always ended up answering a lot of questions about Bennington in general, or even the food.

And of course the waitresses. They were somethin' else. I mean, just to watch them work — they nailed it. They knew where everything was and what they needed to do. And if anybody got out of line, got too loud, they'd let them know. But the waitresses were all part of the Blue Benn cult.

It did get to the point where it was so popular, almost too popular. I'll be working here all day long, whether I'm inside or outside, and I always see someone cross the street into the Vets' Home lawn, taking pictures of the diner. It was almost a daily occurrence.

It's become a Bennington, even a Vermont, insti-

"Cyrus & Ida" cartoon by Matthew Perry
The Vermont News Guide, March 11, 1996

tution. There's just been so much talk about it over the years. And again, I'd get people pulling in out front all the time asking "Where's the Blue Benn Diner?"

For us it's worked out so well. People would drop off their vehicles, go over to the Blue Benn, come back, pick them up, and off they went. For that alone, we're really missing them right now.

But for me the thing I'll miss the most is just seeing everyone there. Every time I went to the Benn I would always run into somebody I knew. Always. I'd walk in there, and I'd go right down the line; people would say hi to me; I'd say hi to them and have a quick conversation with all kinds of people before I even sat down. [*laughs*] Everybody seemed to be on the same page. Everybody was — well, it was a cool place. For a lot of us going there was an experience, not just going to the diner.

William Fisk & Cinda Morse

Romantics

At some point in the interview, the conversation veers off in an unusual direction. "Remember the time we were out in Monterey, California, at that conference and we got talking about homogenization?" Cinda reacts to the question with a nod. They are a couple that likes a deep dive into a subject and, after 20 years together, can easily follow each other's shifting trains of thought. He's 75 and a retired attorney, she's 73 and a retired nonprofit administrator. Together they're a formidable pair and, on occasion, quite a romantic one.

Bill: I'm an attorney and a certified public accountant. I'm retired.

Cinda: Nonprofit administrator is what I have done all my life. I'm now retired. I worked at The Tutorial Center, the Better Bennington Corporation, and my last gig was at Oak Hill Children's Center, in Pownal.

I'm curious about your Valentine's Day date at the Blue Benn. I've been told the story by one of the waitresses working that night. Can you tell me your version? [See waitress Heidi Tilley's version of the story on page 39.]

Bill: [*laughs*] We've been together since 1990. We were married on December 19, 1998. I think it was probably somewhere in there, right?

Cinda: That sounds right. We were still romantic then, so probably. [*laughs*]

Bill: You might say we were living in sin at that point. [*laughs*]

Cinda: We always have these debates — "Should we go out to dinner for Valentine's Day?" "No, every place will be crowded, we won't get in — back and forth." So we finally decided to try the Blue Benn, figuring most people would go to fancier places. Since it was Valentine's Day, we thought we'd bring our own candle in a candlestick, and that would be our romantic Valentine. So we arrived with the candle. Nobody much was there; maybe one or two other people just finishing.

Bill: We got there late-ish. Somewhere around seven. [*laughs*] We were in a good mood by the time we got there. We'd brought the candlestick along — I can't recall whose idea it was, Cinda's or mine — but anyway, we brought it along, and we asked them, "Is it OK?" And they thought it was great, so we lit it up on the table. And we were sitting in the window, so people going by could see us.

Cinda: It was the last booth to the north.

Bill: Yeah, it was on the north side; to the right when you walk in.

Cinda: We checked to see if it was OK, if we weren't too late. Sharon thought the candle was cool, so she was happy to let us in. When we sat down they turned the overheard lights down, and when the other people who were still there left, they locked the door. We had the whole diner to ourselves. And they were great. [*laughs*] It was so fun!

Huevos Rancheros
Jim Woodward

Bill: What we had for diner? [*laughs*] The waitresses could probably tell you better than I could. If I had to guess, I'd say hash and eggs or something crazy like that. You like that …

Cinda: A garden scramble. …

They probably did a dessert thing for us. We used to eat Indian pudding all the time. We ate a lot of Indian pudding.

Bill: Warmed up and always with ice cream. …

We didn't ask for music; Sharon just went over and fired up the jukebox, and we started hearing "romantic" music. It was cool. Mostly oldies stuff — love songs. Maybe Frankie Valli? Not that I was a fan. And they always had "Moonlight in Vermont," the Willie Nelson version, so they probably played that.

Cinda: We danced. We were in a phase where we were doing ballroom dancing with Barbara Roan. She used to do classes; she and Danny Michaelson did ballroom dancing classes. So we used to practice.

Bill: Both of us have a sense of humor, so how could we resist? There'd be an element of yucking it up a little bit. "Let's just camp this out for what it's worth." So we were doing that, dancing in the aisle.

I know someone else came, and they knocked on the door, and the waitresses said they were closed. [*laughs*] So they preserved exclusivity for us for the evening, so that was great. [*laughs*]

We did it as a fun thing, and it was really fun, and they were really so nice. I think we all had a good time, Sharon and Heidi too, making the whole night really fun. They were always super ladies. My big worry is I hope I left a good tip that night! [*laughs*]

We've been regulars at the Blue Benn for years. Well, Cinda more than me. You were going there longer than we were together.

Cinda; That's true. I've gone there since I was in Bennington. I came here in '78 or '79. Bill came in '80, but we didn't meet for another 10 years or so. My two kids grew up here and going to the Benn was always kind of a special treat for them. I take my grandkids there now.

There were a couple of things that made us regulars. The food's great, and it was a really varied menu, which was always interesting. Probably the less traditional stuff appealed to me more than the typical diner food. And the other thing that was really fun about it was, everybody went there. It was a real cross section of the community.

I liked that there was an honor system. I thought that was really nice. People arrived, and there was a code of conduct. If you were waiting for a booth, you sat in the vestibule. Nobody took your name, you knew who came in, you knew who you were before and who you were after, and everybody took their turns. If someone came into the vestibule and walked right in, somebody would explain the ground rules to them. [*laughs*] If not, the waitresses always minded the store, they always knew who was next in line. [*laughs*]

Bill: No, it wasn't exactly the kind of place where you could slip a hundred-dollar bill to the maître d'. [*laughs*]

It was just neat to go there; it had a club or a pub-like atmosphere. You expected, if you walked into the Blue Benn when it was busy, you'd know at least one or two people in there.

I'd go to the Blue Benn, and run into a superior court judge, or the sheriff, or all kinds of tradespeople. …

Cinda: Or the deer hunters who were up bright and early in the morning and there for breakfast. …

But it was also the staff, who really made that happen, because they knew people's names, and they always said hello; they were always friendly; they remembered your kids. And I have a feeling that's one of the reasons that tourists, if they landed there, came back again, because it was such a warm, friendly, community place. And at some level, they knew this is a happening place in Bennington.

Bill [*laughs*]: What's the old joke? Drive by the Blue Benn and see … who's having breakfast together on Sunday morning. Well, something like that. [*laughs*] Anything that happens at the Blue Benn you might as well post it on the community bulletin board.

The waitresses knew Cinda, and they knew me. I remember one time I was in there for lunch with an attorney I worked with, a woman. We sat down — I don't know if we sat down in a booth or at the counter, but Sharon blasts out for the benefit of everybody in the room, "Hey, that's not your wife!" [*laughs*]

So I had to go through the whole explanation — "This is a fellow attorney." [*laughs*] I'll always remember that. Sharon — that was great. So I looked at the woman, my colleague, and I said, "I'm sorry, but this is THE place." She hadn't been there before.

Cinda: OK, I'm on a different tangent here, but listening to this conversation and thinking about the Blue Benn, I want to say that I hope Mary Lou knows how important the diner was to all of us and how much they contributed to the community. It makes me think of the movie *It's a Wonderful Life*. You don't know what an impact someone or something has on a town, until it goes away. And then, all of a sudden, you realize that this really is an important thread in our community and that it's been there, in the background, helping bring us together for a long time.

Jukebox
Jim Woodward

Rick Martell & Elaine Lembo

Romantics

It started over French toast at the counter of the Blue Benn. Neither knew then — the lumberjack and the journalist —that they shared a dream of buying a boat and sailing off into the horizon. A diner in a landlocked state seems an unlikely spot for two seafaring adventurers to meet, but fate can have a funny sense of humor. In a Hollywood scriptwriter's hands their first encounter would make the perfect "meet-cute." And like the end of any good Rom-Com, the final scene played out as hoped: Rick and Elaine bought a 38-foot schooner and "sailed the world over." Thirty years later, they're still on the water, looking out at the waves from a captain's house on Prudence Island, Rhode Island, where Elaine writes and Rick creates beautiful wood-fired pottery

.

Rick: I'm 77, coming up on 78. I spent about 30 years sailing. Now I work on my art. I'm still doing clay work.

Elaine: I'm 61. Rick sailed boats as a delivery skipper and a project engineer for many years. And we owned our own boat, "Land's End" [an oak-framed Crocker ketch from 1935].

Sailing is something that was always inside of me; I don't come from a sailing family at all. As a matter of fact, I was born in Philadelphia and raised in Pittsburgh. But I always wanted to sail, from the time I was a child and dreamed of the sea. First it was just a dream. And then I pursued it. I was persistent and obsessive, and even though I always wanted to be a writer, I thought I always wanted to live on a boat, eat fish, and write about people on islands.

After graduating from Penn State, I went to the *Washington Post* as a clerk, because we were all inspired by Woodward and Bernstein. I used my clip file [published articles] from the *Post* to get hired as a reporter at *The Vineyard Gazette* on Martha's Vineyard. I beat them into submission and made them hire me. [*laughs*] I spent five years there. Everybody who was anybody in the literary scene passed through the *Gazette*. That afforded me a great file of profiles of people like, oh god, Beverly Sills, Lady Bird Johnson, Ted Kennedy, the Styrons, Alfred Eisenstaedt, who became a personal friend. So yeah, I had this kind of crazy existence there. But all good things come to an end, and when it was time to move on to the small daily, I chose the *Bennington Banner*, and Wendy Severinghaus hired me.

Rick: At that time, I was living in North Bennington. I'd decided a few years back to go into the logging business [*a big change from his previous occupation: professional skipper*]. I was still doing boat things, but I was also logging.

Elaine: Vermont was a big change for me as well. I loved Vermont, I thought it was gorgeous, but it was a truly traumatic episode, moving so far from the ocean. That's how Rick comes into it.

It was a beautiful blue, bursting blue Sunday in September, and we all took off for the Blue Benn. Of course,

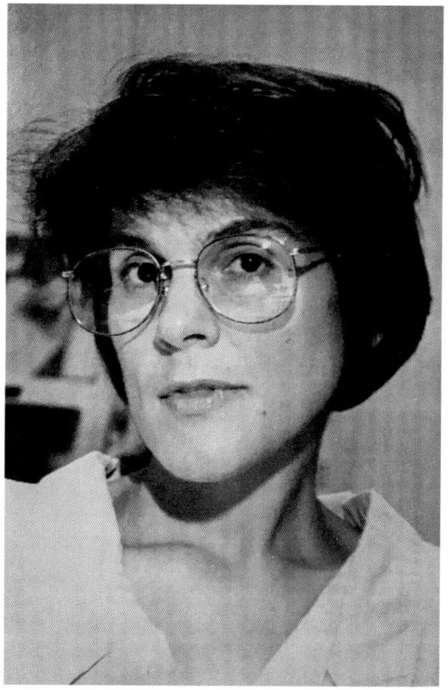

Elaine Lembo, 1990
The Bennington Banner

Opposite: Aboard the ketch "Land's End"
Billy Black

Rick Martell
People of Vermont postcard, 1986
Inscribed "To All My Friends at the Benn, Rick"

Opposite: The Don Sawyer watercolor that hangs in Elaine and Rick's kitchen

it was packed — typical Sunday. There was only room at the counter. Now I was into matchmaking at that point and I was fixing up a friend from the Vineyard with a woman from Petersburgh, New York. So the woman sat at the counter on the other side of the pass-through — that little counter thing Brenda and all the girls would lift up to get behind the counter. I wanted my matches to sit together, so I sat on the other side of the pass-through. The person sitting next to me was Rick.

Rick: Well, the Blue Benn was always the place to go for Sunday brunch and always packed. That was in 1990.

Elaine: It was either '90 or '91. I left the Vineyard in October of 1990, so it would've been probably '91. I had just moved there in fall of '90. And so in fall of '91, I met Rick at the Blue Benn, and truly, the conversation that took place there was what set us off on our dream, our multifaceted dream. He wrote a letter to me, after that crazy conversation.

Rick: Hah! That's right. [*laughs*]

Elaine: Well, he was sitting next to me, and I had ordered one of Sonny's stellar, calorically laden, strawberry cream-cheese French toast dishes. I haven't eaten anything like that in 30 years. But anyway, I ordered it. And there's Rick sitting next to me, wearing a pink sleeveless T-shirt, and his John Lennon-esque sunglasses, with his biceps flashing this prehistoric rabbit tattoo. He's sitting there eating two eggs, sunny-side up that he's cutting up. I can feel him looking at me. I have a Sunday *New York Times* with me, and I can feel his eyes looking at me. So I turned to him and I said, "It's a big newspaper. Would you like some of it?" And he looked over and said, "No, no, no, no, no, no, no."

I turned to him and I said, "I just ordered strawberry cream-cheese French toast, and I'm going to eat the whole thing." And he just went, "Uh…" Then I said, you know, "It's gonna be a good meal." And then, eventually, he got it together to turn to me and say, "Do you live around here?"

Finally I admitted I worked at the *Bennington Banner* as the arts editor. He said, "I thought Wendy was the arts editor." I freaked out a bit at that, because I thought, oh god, small New England town, here we go again. Everybody knows everybody. I asked him how he knew Wendy and he said, "Well, I used to have a clay studio in Williamstown." I had no idea what the hell he was talking about. Here I am, the arts editor, with no idea what a clay studio is. "Yeah, I showed in galleries," and da-de-da-de-da. He goes on and tells me about his career as an artist, which I had no idea what he was talking about. [*laughs*]

And then he says, "But I've just gotten divorced, and I'm selling my house, and I'm sailing away." I said, "Wow … I just moved here from Martha's Vineyard, and I really have to say, for as beautiful as Vermont is, it's days like this when I really miss the ocean." He just looked at me and said, "Really?"

We ate our meals and continued our chitchat and then he got up to leave. I thought to myself — I kid you not — "I haven't seen the last of that person." And two things came over me at once. One was, "Wow, what an interesting guy." And the other was, "Don't go anywhere near it." [*laughs*]

Rick: I had pretty much the same hunch. I thought she was a — well, I just knew that she was a very interesting and talented woman. And I wanted to get to know her. I had no other way of getting ahold of her. She never even told me her name.

Elaine: He wrote me a letter on this beautiful handmade paper and quoted John Masefield's poem "Sea Fever" in the letter, about going down to the sea and asked if I would go out to dinner with him. And he gave me his phone number.

Rick: I had to go and buy a *Banner* and find out who the arts editor was. That's who I wrote the letter to. [*laughs*]

Elaine: When I was working at the *Banner*, you got to take dinner sometime between five and seven. If Rick was getting off work — he doesn't remember this [*laughs*] — he would drive over there —

Rick: Well, they weren't open for dinner every night.

Elaine: True, but when they were open and he was on his way home from work, we would meet there for dinner. I'd have carrot soup and brown rice. He'd always left the log truck running outside.

Rick: You didn't shut diesels off, especially in the winter. For me the Blue Benn had always been a regular thing, even way back. I used to go there all the time. If you wanted to meet somebody in Bennington, that was the place you met them.

I'd say two things about the diner: the Blue Benn changed as soon as *The New York Times* did an article on it. It got too popular and too touristy. Although it was a good show to watch how confused they were waiting to get a booth. [*laughs*] I also want to say that I've been to a lot of diners, all over the States, and the Blue Benn is probably the best of all them.

Elaine: To this day, in our kitchen, we have a framed portrait of the Blue Benn. We found the artwork at Hemmings [*Motor News* and gas station] and I said, "Oh, I have to have this for posterity." So I bought it, we framed it beautifully, and it's still on our kitchen wall.

I miss a lot of things about Vermont. When we left we sold everything, Rick's house, the log truck, everything, and I just quit the *Banner.* We bought our schooner — that was our mission: buying a boat to sail away over the horizon.

Rick: I miss the Blue Benn, for sure. I miss the camaraderie, the people, the food, the banter that goes back and forth. It was just a great place to be — like *Cheers* without the booze. [*laughs*]

Marie-Pierre Huguet & Sandy Sumner

Romantics

Their life stories could hardly be more mismatched. A woodworker from Pittsburgh, Sandy Sumner came to Vermont via Queens, "needing a soft place to land." Marie-Pierre Huguet ditched her university studies in France to come to America, determined to master the nuances of American English. But a few minutes into conversation with the couple and their connection is obvious: it comes down to mechanics. They both relish the mechanics of design; one applies it to construction, the other to designing university course work. "We approach creativity in the same way. We're very disciplined about it," says Sandy. "Very methodical," Marie-Pierre chimes in. "We have very similar processes. Mine is just in education, and Sandy's is in wood."*

Sandy: I was born in New Jersey and raised in Pittsburgh, Pennsylvania. I hated school, wanted to be in construction and ended up working for myself. I'd spent my summers up here at camp, and I was very close with my uncle and aunt, here in Bennington. In 1985, I decided to move to Bennington — I was 35 at the time. I'd always wanted to get back to Vermont.

Marie-Pierre: I ended up here by accident. I was a student in France. I was working on a project with no funding, about teaching English as a foreign language to adults. We wanted to be authentic, we wanted a piece about American English, not just all the British English stuff. So I decided to take a sabbatical from my studies, and come to America. So I came over to work as a private teacher for a family in Old Bennington who were home-schooling their kids to send them to a French-speaking school in Switzerland. I came to Vermont, fell in love with Vermont and so I stayed.

Sandy: We had mutual friends who one night decided to invite us over for dinner. We hit it off beautifully. [*smiling*]

Marie-Pierre: We met, and I stayed forever, right? [*laughing*]

I started as a teacher of French, of course, at Hoosick Falls Central. I was there for seven years. But what I really like about teaching are the mechanics of it. I love to figure out how to teach someone who doesn't want to learn. So I worked for GE [General Electric] for three years, as an instructional designer. … Now I work for a company based in Texas, designing online courses for universities and colleges, which is perfect for me.

When we first started seeing each other, Sandy was determined to introduce me to a lot of American things I hadn't been exposed to …

Sandy: Food trucks. … Things like going up in the Bennington monument, visiting the deer park. Bennington is quaint. And the Blue Benn is the quaintest. It's magical.

Marie-Pierre: Let's rewind, because I want to talk about the first time I went into the Blue Benn. I'd never

Sandy at the Benn, circa 2001
Marie-Pierre Huguet

"You had people wearing thousand-dollar clothing and you had the local tree chopper, in the same place, and nobody cared."
— Marie-Pierre Huguet

been in a diner in my life, so I'll never forget the first time we went. I actually went in with a purpose, instead of just eating: I want to know more about this place. That was in 2001, I'd been in the U.S. about 10, 15 years. So the first time, I remember Sandy all excited — "Oh, I need to take you to the Blue Benn." And I walk in there, and I felt so claustrophobic. [*laughs*] I did. I was like, how many people do you fit in there? And then squish into this table.

Sandy: Those booths were tight.

Marie-Pierre: I'm thinking, people actually want to do this? [*laughs*] You know, I like my space.

Sandy: But once you relaxed and enjoyed the food. ...

Marie-Pierre: Well, the food's good. ... But for me, first there were all kinds of French notions in my head. With French cuisine your plate has to look pretty. And you have to understand that for a French person to actually leave a restaurant with half of their food in a bag — it's appalling. I'd been in the U.S. long enough by then that I was used to ginormous portions. But I had to get used to the idea of getting two meals out of one, to the idea of a doggy bag. In the Blue Benn, that's how it was.

At the beginning, I tried to go through the entire menu, just to try everything, because I wanted the full experience. [*laughs*] It never happened, because before you know it, you end up with your favorites, and forget the rest.

Sandy: The huevos rancheros.

Marie-Pierre: I had three favorites: fish and chips, the gyro sandwich —

Sandy: And I would always go for big breakfasts — huge — I'd do three eggs, sunny-side up, bacon, hash browns. ...

Marie-Pierre: Oh yeah, the breakfast — I loved the waffles. I would break for the real maple syrup. You have to do that.

Sandy: And his veggie burgers —

Marie-Pierre: And Sonny's omelets were — I mean, that's the thing. Like you said, yeah, you have a favorite, but before you know it, you don't have a favorite anymore because you go, "oh yeah, remember that one, or this one?"

I had a rotation between, as I say, at least three. Oh, the spinach melt.

Sandy: Oh yeah —I went through a phase where if I went more than a week or two without a spinach melt, oh my god. And we tried to make them here at home. ...

Marie-Pierre: We tried to make them — it didn't work.

Sandy: Can I interject here? So when I really began to appreciate the Blue Benn was after my first trip to France with Marie-Pierre. Once we got there, we'd stayed with her family, of course, but we did a lot of day trips. And you could not find a casual place to eat, anywhere. We'd go to all these towns, and if you wanted to eat, you'd have to go to a really fine dining restaurant. There was no such thing as a diner or, at that point in 1991, even a McDonald's or fast-food place.

And so the whole time, I'm thinking, can't I just get a huevos rancheros here, or just like, even a couple eggs and a couple slabs of bacon?

Marie-Pierre: It was so funny. We — you were craving your old favorites. And so we go to this café, and he really wanted eggs. And I made him ask for the eggs in French, because I couldn't do it. [*laughing*] And then he wants ketchup!

Sandy: Yeah, ketchup on everything, that's me. [*laughs*]

Marie-Pierre: Remember when we took my parents to the diner? My dad was hilarious. He barely fit in the booth. My dad is a big guy. By then, of course, he had learned about doggy bags. So he was planning his meals around the doggy bag. [*laughs*] He would order what he perceived as the biggest whatever on the menu. [*laughs*]

Sandy: In France, you would never ask for a doggy bag. That was a real culture shock for them. But it didn't take long before they were into the idea, especially your dad. [*laughs*]

For most people — the locals — not only are drawn to the Blue Benn, love the Blue Benn, but are also proud of the Blue Benn for what it was. It was such a unique place. It was definitely a place where cultures mingled.

Marie-Pierre: But didn't clash, and that's why I loved watching all that stuff. I loved that you could tell, oh, that's a local, that's an out-of-towner.

Sandy: Especially when you were in the waiting room, and the conversations. I always had wonderful conversations in the waiting room. Didn't matter who was in there — somebody from the one percent going up to Stowe or Stratton to ski. …

Marie-Pierre: You had people wearing thousand-dollar clothing and you had the local tree chopper, in the same place, and nobody cared. There was none of that "ooh, I'm from out of state." And once in a while, someone would try that on, but that didn't stand a chance, because the entire community within the diner would somehow put them back where they belonged, which is, you're just eating food.

Sandy: Whenever family or friends came through, I was always so proud to take them. There are diners everywhere with really good food. But the Blue Benn was different. Maybe it was because it was so intimate and the music was so dated, and the waitresses would act out a ballet in that tight, tight space where they served. Everything about it was special. And of course, all the recipes on single papers, up above — I was just so proud, because I knew that my friends or family would have a fun, tasty experience.

Hopefully the new owner will be able to capture that same magic — that welcoming, warm sense. That feeling of home.

** William "Sandy" Sumner passed away on August 4, 2021, at the age of 69.*

Mary Ruefle, 1982

Mary Ruefle

Artists

Mary Ruefle, Vermont's poet laureate, doesn't own a computer. Despite her determination to live life "unplugged," or maybe because of it, her career is crowded with honors and awards: a Guggenheim Fellowship, a National Endowment for the Arts Fellowship, the William Carlos Williams Award from the Poetry Society of America and a Whiting Award. She's published 17 volumes of poetry and prose and even a comic book. But before all that, in the late 1970s, Mary was an impoverished artist living in North Bennington. Struggling to publish her work and put food on the table, a meal at Sonny's Blue Benn Diner was an extravagance she couldn't afford. "Maybe that's why I remember the day and meal so clearly," she says of one cherished memory.

I've been wracking my brain trying to remember the year. I'd say it was 1977.

I started going to the Blue Benn even before Sonny and Mary Lou owned it. I was a student at Bennington College — I came here as a freshman in 1971 — and the diner was one of the few places we could go late at night. Back then, before Sonny bought it, the Benn was a kind of ordinary diner with ordinary food, but it was open 24 hours a day, which made it a popular place to go for college students.

By the time I graduated in 1974, Sonny had bought the diner and I had a friend Ellen who was a waitress there. In the late seventies, I was completely broke. I could barely support myself. My first book didn't come out until 1982 and I'd managed to get a couple of poems published in a few magazines, but that was it.

So there I was, no longer a student, 25 years old and I had NO money. I was a broke, clueless, lost poet. One afternoon I walked into the Blue Benn and, I remember this very clearly, I sat at the counter and ordered a cup of coffee. That's all I had money for, a cup of coffee. I was starving and I had no money for food. And when you're at the counter you look around and everyone's being served — well, that's hard when you're really hungry.

Ellen brought me my coffee and said, "Don't you want anything else?" She must have seen me looking at the food down the counter. But I said, "No, I don't have any money," and she said, "Mary, are you hungry?" and I said "Yes." That was when she went back into the kitchen and talked to Sonny. Now, Sonny knew me. I'd gone in there enough that he knew who I was, but he didn't know I was a struggling writer, or even what I did. So when Ellen came back out of the kitchen, she was carrying a big steaming bowl of soup and bread and she said; "This is on Sonny." I've never forgotten that. I was overwhelmed with the kindness.

Years later, there was a 10-year period when I was teaching at the college, when I went to the Blue Benn regularly. I remember going there once — they would always have special homemade pies on the menu — when they had green tomato pie. I'd never had it and my wait-

Reproduction of a Blue Benn booth, featured in the 2017 Bennington College production of Diana Janis' "East Coast Curriculum." / Opposite: Just two of Mary Ruefle's early and mid-career books.

ress, Pat, said she'd made it, so of course I tried it. It was the best pie. I loved it! I told her it was great and she said that it was her grandmother's recipe. So I asked her for the recipe and she said, "Mary, I'll bring it to you." Next time I came in, maybe two weeks later, she apologized for not having the recipe. Her house had burned down and she'd lost it in the fire! Imagine apologizing to me? She was my favorite waitress.

For me, the seventies and the eighties were the great old days for the Blue Benn. It was such a community place back then, when Sonny would be chummy with the customers and come out from the kitchen to ask everyone about the food. It got too popular. The Benn turned into a landmark and a destination for tourists with long wait times to get a booth and lots of people you didn't know.

FIRE AND PIES

Pat Shepard, waitress extraordinaire, responds to Mary Ruefle's memory of a green tomato pie.

I don't remember Mary asking for the green tomato pie recipe, but I did make all kinds of pies. [*laughing*] She's right about losing the recipe in the fire. We lost everything.

It was in March of '86. I was working at the diner, and a lady called the diner and told me that she just heard on the scanner that my house was on fire. Can you imagine calling me at work and telling me my house is on fire?

Oh my god, I panicked. I got in my car and I drove home through a snowstorm. They had the road blocked right off. I had to park in my neighbors' down below me, and a man says, "You're gonna be arrested. You can't park there. You can't go up there." I said, "That's my house, and I'm going." I jumped out of the car, and I ran up there, because my teenage son was in the house. So I'm running up to the house and people are shouting, "You can't go in there," and I'm shouting "My son is in there!" Actually, by then I was crying. Just then, I saw my son, Greg, coming toward me with a fireman's coat on. There he was in this yellow coat with his pajama bottoms on, and he's yelling, "Mom, mom, mom!" Oh my god, all I could think was, "He's OK, the house can go as long as he's OK." And it did. The house burned to the ground. We had to tear it down.

Luckily we had the best insurance adjustor you could ever have. ... We drove to Springfield so we could pick up [the claims] check to start a new house — he told us we'd get it quicker that way. So we had the fire, built a house, and got married [*to her second husband*] all in the same year.

Magi Randall & Rob Sperber

Artists

Onion soup plays a storied role in Magi and Rob's courtship. In fact, you could say it's what brought the artist and the woodworker together in the first place. It began at the Rhode Island School of Design, where Magi was a graduate student and Rob a guest lecturer, invited to demonstrate his redesigned portable saw mill. Impressed with the talk, and presumably the guy, Magi accepted an offer to dinner. When two bowls of steaming soup arrived at the table, she wondered out loud why onion soup was always so hot. "It's insulated by the cheese," Rob replied, without skipping a beat. "I thought that was brilliant. It was such a practical response," Magi says, recalling the exchange. "That's all it took," Rob laughs. "She was easy." Years later, sitting in a booth at the Blue Benn Diner, they would recount the anecdote to their two young daughters, sipping bowls of piping hot soup; onion, of course, topped with gooey insulation. "Diner tales. That was one that got repeated almost every time one of us ordered onion soup," Magi laughs.

Magi: Some of my favorite moments in the Blue Benn were when Sonny would poke his head out from the kitchen. It was a rare treat. We might be in there really early, or even during a snowstorm and Sonny would lean out from the kitchen just to say "hi." For me it was like seeing an artist in his studio. He'd have a bemused look on his face and he was always very humble.

Rob: I always said it was like me in my shop or Maggie in her studio. I don't want anybody else there. I just want to be alone in my shop. I love being there on the weekends; Sonny loved being in the diner at night working on his recipes.

Magi: It felt as if he was deeply into his work, and that he was reclusive — that he was there to create something. So when you did see him, it felt special.

Rob: He really was a sweet and friendly guy. And Mary Lou, she was definitely in charge, definitely the boss. You'd see her clearing tables or filling salt shakers, always busy. She was incredibly hardworking.

Magi: Those two were so hardworking. I remember seeing the angel pin on Mary Lou the first time — it took me a bit to notice it. I thought, oh, I see how Mary Lou and Sonny are connected — they were both very spiritual about the diner, oddly. [*laughs*] But the place did have a very spiritual quality to it, in that it had a way of bringing the town together.

Rob: I started building my shop in October of '87. That's when we started pouring the foundation. We moved here from New Jersey. We were definitely flatlanders, but I remember when I was building the shop — we were digging the trench to put the water line in — and Phil Harrington was in his machine, digging, and I was in the hole, just covered in mud. Phil's assistant is in there with me and looks at me and says, "You're the only person I ever met that came from away, who'd be down in the hole with me."

Magi: Yeah, in Vermont flatlanders have to earn trust.

[Our daughter] Roxy was around one when we moved here and [her sister] Zoë was born here. I don't think we took the kids much when they were babies and acting obstreperous. They would cry and in a place that small it would be a big issue. It was stressful. So we waited and took them when they were a little older. When we did start taking the kids, they loved it. Now it's hard to remember a time when we didn't go regularly.

Rob: The waitresses were great with the kids. One thing I'll always remember about taking the kids to dinner when they were little was Pat giving Zoë a cup of hot chocolate with whipped cream and then an extra cup of whipped cream. Zoë just loved that.

Magi: I'm pretty positive that Bob [Howe] introduced you to the diner in the first place.

Rob: That's probably true. He'd come over to the shop every Saturday morning and we'd go have breakfast. He'd buy me breakfast. He never let me pay. [*laughs*]

Magi: You thought he was brilliant. Was he still running Porta-Brace at that point?

Rob: Oh yeah, he worked there for quite a while after that. Anyhow, Bob and I would eat breakfast together and he'd give me advice about the business and he'd ask me about machines I'd be tinkering with in the shop. Much later, I started having regular lunches with Jeff [Yucht].

Magi: The waitresses? Authentic to the core; that was what was cool about the Benn. It was like a real diner experience, like something out of a Tom Waits song. That's how I thought of it.

Rob: They were great; they were not gonna take any shit from anybody, especially if you came into the diner and tried to push them around or act nasty or superior to any one of them.

Magi: The diner really was a beautiful snapshot of what egalitarianism should be. I loved the way they treated celebrities the same as all their other customers. That's what I mean by egalitarian. They just treated everyone with respect and they expected respect back. That's what they wanted and they deserved it.

Rob: For a while my favorite dish was the white bean chili. Pat would call me at the shop and say, "Hey, we got white bean chicken chili today." I'd say, "OK, I'll be over." [*laughs*] I'd go in there and she'd have a bowl for me.

Gotta tell my favorite Pat story: One year Jeff [Yucht] took me to the diner for breakfast on my birthday. We were sitting in the middle booth, and I'm facing The Tuscan Sunflower, with Jeff on the other side. Pat was our waitress, and I remember ordering a chicken fajita omelet.

So we're talking, waiting for orders to come, when I hear this commotion — I can't see Pat making her way to our booth — but she arrives with my omelet with a lit candle in it, and the whole diner's singing Happy Birthday to me. The whole place was standing, singing Happy Birthday, and I'm going, "Whoa, what's going on?" Then Pat puts down the omelet, looks at me, and says, "Gotcha." [*laughing*]

Magi: The great thing about the diner was that it was such cross section of community. You never knew who you were going to run into, just that you were going to see someone you knew.

I've got to say something about the counters. I love the counters, the way they were worn away.

Rob: That Formica pattern, worn down by elbows on the counter.

Magi: I love that Sonny and Mary Lou respected that and saw the history in it; that the worn Formica was just a beautiful expression of the place. I also love the way they patch-worked the walls — Sonny putting the specials all over the walls. And Mary Lou would try to clean up the beautiful stainless work, but Sonny would end up covering it again. It was somehow both very functional and artistic. [*laughs*]

Rob: He'd put the signs up, and she'd want to take them down. I had a rule that you order whatever you were sitting under. You couldn't decide what to eat? Whatever sign you were sitting under. …

Magi: [*laughs*] That was his rule. Rob would turn to me and say, "Well, you're under shepherd's pie, that's lunch." [*laughter*]

Rob: One of the things I loved about the Blue Benn was that you could answer the question "What do you want to drink?" by saying, "I'll have my usual." And I just love being able to say that and that the waitresses would know exactly what you meant: diluted cranberry juice and fizzy spritzer water. Coming from a metropolitan area where you didn't have that kind of real connection with people in the community, it was something I really valued. It's what I like about living in a small town — the connection, where everyone knows your name and values your friendship.

Magi: It's funny because New Jersey is the land of diners, mega-diners. But they're big, impersonal places. Sonny kept the Blue Benn small and personal. Sonny and Mary Lou were quirky and that's part of what made the diner work so well. But places, like people, have a lifespan. I think the new owner is trying to keep the spirit of the diner alive and, hopefully, he'll make it work in his own way.

Previous and this page, Catastrophe Hats by Magi Randall: "Tornado" and "Tsunami."

Londa Weisman, circa 1980s

Londa Weisman

Artists

We're in Londa Weisman's home in North Bennington. A spiral staircase she designed and built corkscrews through the center of the house — a house filled with sculpture, ceramic, drawings and hand-crafted furniture, much of it made by Londa. She came to Vermont as a Bennington College student, graduating in 1967. A year into a master's degree in sculpture and ceramics, Londa left school to join her brother and friends on an extraordinary adventure — buying and restoring a 90-foot Baltic Schooner to sail around the world. Her three-year journey — a life-changing experience that even today shapes her work — took her from Portsmouth, England, to Spain, the Cape Verde Islands and, finally, Puntarenas, Costa Rica, where she left the group to go back to Bennington and her graduate studies. In the five decades since, Londa has made a life here as an artist, calling Vermont her home no matter where her travels take her.

I came here to go to school at Bennington College in 1963. I wanted to be a beatnik in New York and Bennington had a work term. I thought I could figure out how to turn that into a New York adventure. [*laughs*] It was a liberal arts college where you could major in studio art — one of only two schools in the country with that option. I knew that it might be the track I wanted to be on.

I can't remember when I discovered the Blue Benn, but what I think I remember is that Mary Lou and Sonny got the diner the same year I started my own small business making pottery, which was in 1974. I graduated in '67. I worked at the Bennington Potters for two years, then I did a year of graduate work at the college in ceramics and sculpture, and then I went away to sea for three years. I left for what I thought would be a year, that turned into three years, and came back in 1973. I joined the boat in Portsmouth, England, and I got off three years later in Puntarenas, Costa Rica. After I'd been gone for a few years, the college suggested I might want to think about coming back to finish my graduate degree. I decided it was time to come back. So I left the boat before it crossed the Pacific and went around the world — more than once —before sinking in New Zealand. But that's a story for another time.

Once I came back to Vermont, I was able to set up a studio — Mechanic Street Pottery & Iron Works — to try to earn my living as a potter. I mistakenly thought I would also have enough time to work on sculpture. That came later. And somewhere in there, I discovered the Benn.

One of my more vivid memories is going there with a friend, a man I used to date. There were times when we'd go to the diner three times in one day. But the other thing we used to do fairly frequently was go there late enough so that we were the last or the second-to-the-last people to leave, and Sonny and Mary Lou would put old-timey stuff on the jukebox. They'd be cleaning up, and we'd ask if it was OK to stay a little longer. It was always fine with them — at least, we thought it was fine. And there were a lot of evenings like that. It was just a lovely, really lovely time. Did we ever dance? I can't remember, but we might have in the aisle. [*laughs*]

At some point I started writing before breakfast, for myself, and didn't want to go out for breakfast. So my Blue Benn habits changed and I would frequently have breakfast there at lunchtime. The heyday of my years going to the Blue Benn was when I was on my own — I was working alone, I was living alone, and the people I saw the most were the people at the Benn.

Londa at her studio, 2018

The Blue Benn was the closest thing we had to the quintessential coffee shop where you can go hang out and meet people. What I needed, as a person living and working on my own, was a place I could go and probably run into somebody I would enjoy seeing.

For me, at that time, the Blue Benn was my second home. They would know when I was out of town when nobody else did. I remember at one point during that time, I'd come back from a craft fair with a paper bag full of cash, which I somehow managed to leave in a booth at the Benn. It was a nondescript bag that had papers and all the checks, and a lot of cash. The diner was closed by the time I realized what I'd done, but I didn't worry about it. I knew I would pick it up when they opened. Of course they had it, sitting under the register.

I was famous for leaving leftovers. I would always take my leftovers home, and half the time I would forget them and they would come running out with them. I mean, they took care of me. I think that's how I'd put it. I felt taken care of when I was there. And the way I was living, it was a big deal. There are friendships that are situational, and that was definitely the case. But what's been wonderful for me is how the friendship with Mary Lou has turned into something far more. She's an essential friend now.

In 1999, Sid and I fell in love very abruptly and very completely, much to my surprise. I say that because he was not on my list of the kind of person I was looking for. I definitely wasn't looking for an older man. I definitely wasn't looking for a businessman. I wasn't looking for a Republican. But falling in love — if you fall in love that way, you don't turn it down. You can't.

Anyhow, at some point I said, "If they don't like you at the Benn, we probably have to call this off." [*laughs*] "And if you don't like the Benn, it's gonna be a real problem." So we went to the Benn, and it worked out just fine. Before that ever happened I'd have real conversations with Pat [Sheppard] or Mary Lou or Lisa about what was happening in my life. I started talking to the three of them about Sid when that relationship started. And when I finally came in with Sid, Mary Lou walked over and said, "I want to see the person who put the smile on her face." It was great.

My relationship with Mary Lou is very surprising. My friendship with her is something that I cherish immensely, in large part because she is exactly what she is. What she is on the outside is what she is on the inside. There's a transparency there, and I find the people I'm closest to have that quality. But I'm also grateful to her for how incredibly kind she's been. What was singular at the Benn was the variety of deep conversations that took place there. It all felt genuine, not necessarily cheerful, but always very real.

There was a point when I would tell people, "If the Blue Benn closes, I'll leave town." [*laughs*] Now I'm more open minded. If [the sale had happened] 15 years ago, I would have been distraught. If it were more than 21 years ago, I would have been tearing my hair out. Losing the Benn would've felt absolutely unbearable.

Now I think yes, there's a loss that an institution that was very much about the people who owned it and ran it isn't owned and run by them anymore. But it's part of the whole wheel that we're on that's life. It would be wonderful if the old-slash-new Benn became its own iconic institution. There's never gonna be another Sonny. There's never gonna be another Mary Lou. And nobody should try to be those things. But if we're lucky, another original has come along.

Spiral staircase by Londa Weisman
Londa Weisman

Mary Lou and Lisa, circa 1980s

Scott Dundas

Outdoorsmen

Scott Dundas says his most enduring memory of Sonny's Blue Benn was of the first moment he set foot in the place nearly 36 years ago. A lanky 14-year-old, Scott had never before been in a diner. His parents preferred to take their two children to restaurants with cloth napkins where they could claim a quiet table, hoping to escape the inevitable patient or ex-patient of his doctor father asking "just one small question." But once Scott crossed the Blue Benn's threshold, he never looked back. "I just remember thinking the whole thing was just so cool," he chuckled. One of the diner's steadfast regulars — even a hiatus away from Bennington couldn't keep him entirely away from the Blue Benn — Scott pegs people's need for diners to nostalgia. "One of the few things that you can count on in people is nostalgia. Diners are nostalgic … they're a throwback to a gentler time."

I moved to Bennington in 1970 when I was four. No, both my parents were New Englanders. My mother was from New Hampshire and my father was from Massachusetts. I was born in Ohio, so I don't consider myself a Vermonter. As they say, true Vermonters are born and bred here.

We lived on the outskirts of town, so yeah, I think I had the best of everything — surrounded by nature and

Justus Taylor
Courtesy Carla Lund

rural living, but then close enough to town so I could jump on my bike and go visit with friends. All the outdoor stuff, skiing and hiking, all became second nature to us.

I left Bennington for about 16 years, living in northern Vermont. I came back in 2004 and I was a landscaper-gardener for a lot of years; now I work as a property manager on a 40-acre estate. It's been seven years and it's been wonderful. Every day is different, so I never really know what the next thing will be.

The first time I ever went to the Blue Benn, I was probably 14. So that would've been in 1984. Justus Taylor took me to lunch there. Justus was an old hippie. He moved to Vermont from Greenwich Village in the sixties and opened a sandal shop at Potters Yard. [*Potters Yard is a four-acre Bennington property with two historic buildings, a 1922 grist mill and a nineteenth-century one-room schoolhouse on site.*] He was an amazing craftsman and was actually pretty famous. If you have a pair of his sandals, today they'd be a pretty hot item.

My memory of the eighties was that Bennington, particularly the downtown area, was pretty thriving, at least compared to now. There was just a lot going on — a lot of shops and a lot of people came to go shopping in Bennington.

I was in high school in the eighties — I graduated in '88, from Mount Anthony — and the Blue Benn Diner was always filled with Bennington College students. I always had the impression that the college wanted to be separate from the town. But I will say that back then half the diner was filled with Bennington College students.

Back then the students were always kind of funky — they just stood out, you know? They were just different. They were just such artists, and they all seemed to come from urban settings, so you could just, like, whoa! That person stands out. But it was neat. The diner was such a great place back then — it was so vibrant. It might've been the most popular place in Bennington. I don't know when it lost that feeling, but I would say in the nineties.

When I was in high school, we used to go there a lot on weekends, and the line would be out the door and down the steps and around the turn. You'd wait an hour to have breakfast, and that was just fine — nobody complained, because it was that good. And on weekdays, it was full, but there wasn't a line, but it just was full. Like at lunch, if you went there in the eighties or the early nineties, a lot of workmen were there in the morning for breakfast, at five or six o'clock. Over the past few years, that's just disappeared. Now there are no workpeople there, it's almost all elderly people. I'd look around at the clientele and I'd, think, "Where did the work guys — where do they go now?" It could be that they don't work, because there is no work. [*laughs*]

And when I was in high school, Sonny was there every day, all day. Well, he got there at like three in the morning and worked until lunch, one or two, and then somebody else would take over. But he was there every day. And he was cooking — he was like, in the back, cooking. He really made the diner what it was — his attention to detail, his personality. He knew everybody in Bennington. People would come in, he'd be in the back room with that little window, and you could see him cooking, and people would be like, "Hey, Sonny! Sonny!" and he'd shout, "Hello, Joe! How's it going, Joe?" — greeting everybody that came in that door or at least anybody that was somebody from Bennington did that. [*laughs*] That's all he gave you, was like, "Hey, Joe, how's it going?" He didn't come out and chat with people, because he was busy. He was really working. And he worked hard.

When Sonny slowed down, that's when the Blue Benn Diner kind of slowed down with him — that and the economy of Bennington changed as well. Things got a little harder here. I think people who had extra money to go out became a little more scarce. The bypass was a factor too.

Before they put the bypass in, all the traffic from Route 7 went by the Blue Benn Diner, Routes 7 and 9 were major corridors, and Route 7 especially for the skiers going through town. If they were headed to Bromley or Stratton or Killington [ski resorts], they would go right by the Blue Benn Diner. Now they don't. [*shrugs*]

I want to add that the Blue Benn's success wasn't just about Sonny. Mary Lou was there every day. She knew everybody. She worked her ass off. And all the waitresses knew everybody. And they worked their asses off. And Lisa was great — they all just chipped in. It wasn't just Sonny.

The waitresses, yeah they were pretty sassy. [*laughs*] And I gave it right back to them, so it was fun. I think the best way to put it is that I've always gotten along with all of them and really liked most of them. They're like sisters. Every one of them had their style, and each had their customers that really liked them. So you'd see people come in the door, and head to one side of the diner or the other depending on which side Brenda or Sharon or Pat was working.

Pat stood out as one of my favorite people. She's just a wonderful person, and I've always admired how hard she works. Out of all the waitresses there, she never stops. They all are good, hard workers, but watching her; she's filling salt shakers, she's scrubbing the coffee pot, she's putting coffee cups out. I mean, it doesn't stop, with her. I was so impressed just watching her work. And then she's just a nice, kind person, too.

I can remember, again back when I was in high school, when the waitresses would smoke at work. There was a blue haze of smoke settled at the top of the ceiling. Half the people who ate there would be smoking, and all the waitresses were smoking — they'd put their cigarettes in an ashtray on the counter and wait on the tables — it's incredible to think about that now, [*laughs*] everybody smoked, [*laughs*] that's just how it was.

We'd all go there from high school, a group of four or five of us and take over two booths with a chair in the aisle, and just be totally obnoxious teenagers. I'm sure everybody hated us for it. [*laughs*] And of course we'd all be smoking cigarettes with people eating in the next booth. [*laughs*] When Sonny instituted the no-smoking rule it was huge.

Probably my most fixed memory of the diner was the first time I went there. Sharon was my waitress and I was 14 years old. So, like I said earlier, Justus Taylor invited me and my friend Ethan Shrier to lunch. His stepfather was Terry Ehrich, and Justus and Terry Ehrich were best buddies. So one day, Justus was like, "Come on, kids. Let's go to the Blue Benn Diner." And we went with him.

Of course, he knew everybody, including Sonny. We walked in, and we sat at the counter — left side, like halfway in the middle. It was crowded. Once we're in the door Justus is yelling, "Hey, Sonny! Hey, Pat! Hey,

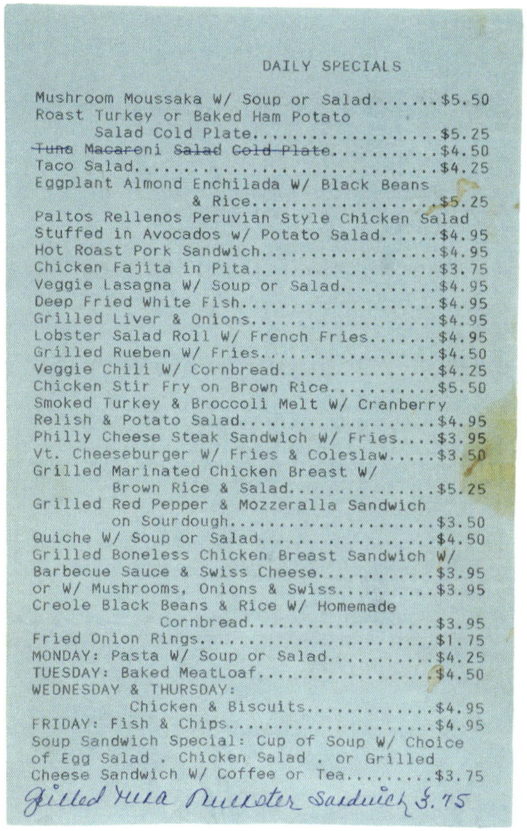
DAILY SPECIALS

Mushroom Moussaka W/ Soup or Salad.......$5.50
Roast Turkey or Baked Ham Potato
Salad Cold Plate...................$5.25
~~Tuna~~ ~~Macaroni~~ ~~Salad~~ ~~Cold Plate~~...........$4.50
Taco Salad.............................$4.25
Eggplant Almond Enchilada W/ Black Beans
& Rice...................$5.25
Paltos Rellenos Peruvian Style Chicken Salad
Stuffed in Avocados w/ Potato Salad......$4.95
Hot Roast Pork Sandwich..................$4.95
Chicken Fajita in Pita...................$3.75
Veggie Lasagna W/ Soup or Salad..........$4.95
Deep Fried White Fish....................$4.95
Grilled Liver & Onions...................$4.95
Lobster Salad Roll W/ French Fries.......$4.95
Grilled Rueben W/ Fries..................$4.50
Veggie Chili W/ Cornbread................$4.25
Chicken Stir Fry on Brown Rice...........$5.50
Smoked Turkey & Broccoli Melt W/ Cranberry
Relish & Potato Salad....................$4.95
Philly Cheese Steak Sandwich W/ Fries....$3.95
Vt. Cheeseburger W/ Fries & Coleslaw.....$3.50
Grilled Marinated Chicken Breast W/
Brown Rice & Salad..............$5.25
Grilled Red Pepper & Mozzeralla Sandwich
on Sourdough....................$3.50
Quiche W/ Soup or Salad..................$4.50
Grilled Boneless Chicken Breast Sandwich W/
Barbecue Sauce & Swiss Cheese............$3.95
or W/ Mushrooms, Onions & Swiss..........$3.95
Creole Black Beans & Rice W/ Homemade
Cornbread..................$3.95
Fried Onion Rings........................$1.75
MONDAY: Pasta W/ Soup or Salad...........$4.25
TUESDAY: Baked MeatLoaf..................$4.50
WEDNESDAY & THURSDAY:
Chicken & Biscuits.............$4.95
FRIDAY: Fish & Chips.....................$4.95
Soup Sandwich Special: Cup of Soup W/ Choice
of Egg Salad, Chicken Salad, or Grilled
Cheese Sandwich W/ Coffee or Tea.........$3.75
Grilled Tuna Muenster Sandwich 3.75

Menu, circa 1980s

Customer comment card, front and back

Ransom Gore, farm manager, pre–smoking ban, circa 1970s

Sharon!" Everybody said, "Hello, Justus! Great!" And it was just the coolest experience. I remember thinking the whole thing was just like a whole other level of dining that I never knew anything about. My parents would never go to a place like that, not because they're snobs; my father is a doctor and I think he got tired of dealing with patients and ex-patients every time he went out. All these questions about their health and their prescriptions. He just wanted a quiet table in the corner, so they would take us to fancier restaurants where it was harder to intrude.

It's funny, I don't remember thinking the food in the Benn was like, ah! THE best burger I ever had!, or anything like that. It was good, but what I loved was the atmosphere. I remember Sharon — she must have been around eighteen — and she was tough. She was so strong. You could just tell, this girl took nothing from anybody, you know? You could just see she had such personal inner strength. Here I am this skinny 14-year-old and I'm thinking, god, this girl is so tough. She was smoking cigarettes too, sometimes even while they were serving you, the waitresses had a cigarette going. There was always an ashtray right there, and they'd turn around and take a hit and then ask you what you wanted, and blow smoke in your face. [*laughs*] Like something out of a 1940s movie.

The whole experience just blew me away. I just thought it was so cool. I just never stopped going after that, it was just a pretty great experience. Since then until Covid, I've probably eaten there thousands of times. [*laughs*] It wasn't unusual for me to go there three times a week. That was the last restaurant I went to, right before lock down. I was in there with two other people and we were talking about Covid and how scary it was getting. I was thinking to myself, "Well, this is it. I'm gonna enjoy this, because I'm not coming back for a long time." Looking back, it's ironic that I thought that with no idea a year later Sonny's Blue Benn Diner would be sold.

Michael Foster

Outdoorsmen

Ten feet above the ground, from the cabin of his New Holland tractor, Michael Foster looks out on a better world. "There's a lot of beauty to see when you're cutting, looking out over the views; the mountains and the wide open fields … places where I've spent my life," he says. Most of the time, he stays focused on the job at hand with the risk of breaking expensive equipment always on his mind. A gearbox alone costs $2,000. But when an open field stretches out before him and music flows from the tractor's built-in speakers, Michael — farmer, landscaper and conservationist — gets a chance to reflect. "You can think about your next job, your last job, what you're gonna do next, where you're going. Sometimes I think about the people I've known, my dad, my brother. Sometimes I just think about life."

I'm 63 and have lived in Vermont most of my life. I grew up on a 200-acre farm in North Pownal, which I inherited from my father. Today I own two farms. Two farms and no animals, not even a goldfish.

What do I do? That's not so easy to answer. On my tax returns I've had to think about whether to identify as a farmer or landscaper. In the end, I said I was a landscaper, because for about 40 years I've been working on conservation projects, designed to keep land open and eradicate

invasives like multiflora and honeysuckle brush. I've done about 2,000 acres per year of environmental clearing.

I started going to Sonny's Blue Benn about 12 years ago, maybe a little longer than that. I probably went there the first time with Julius [Rosenwald]. He was the one who got me started doing a lot of the conservation work. Julius encouraged and inspired me.

I'd usually go to lunch at the diner about once a month with Julius or a customer of mine. I'd go early between 11 and 12 to try and beat the crowds. If I'd go for breakfast, I'd usually go alone and to dinner with my wife, sometime in the evening when they weren't busy. Mostly I'd go for lunch and they would always know what I wanted. I would always get a spinach melt. If you could imagine two dinner plates put together, and inside would be spinach, mushrooms, onions, and alfalfa sprouts.

That's what I liked about going there, it wasn't just a lot of fried food; they had other food, healthy stuff that wasn't just a regular garden salad. And the spinach melt was one of the healthy things that you could get. Or you could get baked scrod for dinner. For breakfast, I'd usually have the French toast or scrambled eggs. It would depend on what I was going to be doing for the day. If I went there in the morning for breakfast, it was because I might've anticipated a harder day, using a chainsaw, clearing land. I'd want a good high-energy breakfast.

There are probably close to 700 internet reviews on the Blue Benn, and 90 percent of them are good. The 10 percent of them that are negative, I would have to say, come from people having to wait. Maybe there's a car show or something happening a couple of towns over and they decide to stop. So people would come, there would be a long line, they would get antsy about it; and then, of course, they would be bombarded in the kitchen and the waitresses caught heck for all this, and sometimes they didn't deal with it well.

In Vermont there's a saying — "If you gonna mess with the bull, you're gonna get the horns." In a lot of places, they say the customer is right. But not in Vermont. [*laughs*] If you're wrong, you're wrong, and they're gonna let you know it. And that's the way they were, I think, at the Blue Benn.

My favorite waitress was Heidi. She's my cousin and let's just say, she is definitely a native Vermonter. [*laughs*] When my dad was sick — he had bone cancer — we'd usually go to the diner for lunch if he had a doctor's appointment. I used to take him to the doctor's when he was very ill, usually two, three times a week, and so we would go down there quite a bit. He liked seeing Heidi there; she's his brother's daughter. Sometimes we'd just talk about our day, nothing important, just being together. Of course, everyone at the counter is close to you; they have their back to you, so I don't think they're really listening, or maybe they are. Still, I always felt like I could talk there.

Of course, I miss the food and I miss seeing people I know there. It was place where you'd walk in, and someone would say, "Come over and have lunch with us," or whatever. Or you'd walk up to the counter and talk to them for a minute or two; because it was close, you didn't want to stand there forever in the aisle and speak with them. I'll also miss just watching the scene, the passersby, the people that come in for lunch or dinner. Sometimes you'd try to listen to them, sometimes it was just fun to watch the world go by.

Mowing

Michael Biddy

Outdoorsmen

Michael Biddy had his heart set on moving to Vermont since high school. It took him a few years to get here — driving a Ford pickup truck through a blinding snowstorm. "I arrived in this beautiful '56 Ford with no running boards, painted flat black, spare tire on the front as a cattle guard, and a camper on the back, with eagle stencils on the doors. I bought it for two hundred bucks." Raised in Connecticut, it was Vermont's rugged countryside and snowy winters that lured him north. That was 1971, when you could share an apartment, since condemned as a toxic waste site, for $15 a month. "In those days I was a long-haired college graduate. Not a hippie. Hippies got checks from somewhere every month." Fifty-one years on, Michael is every bit the Vermonter.

I didn't have the privilege to be born in Vermont. I chose to come here.

I visited Vermont in high school, as part of a ski trip. I looked around at the beautiful landscape and the mountains, going to the ski area, and thought, "I'm gonna live there" — I made that decision early on. I moved here permanently in 1971, just about this time of year [February]. That was the winter there was four feet of snow on the roofs in the mountains and buildings were

Michael Biddy, 1983

collapsing because of it. I remember driving up here in a storm. I had to rescue a few people on the way. I had the right vehicle — snow tires and a heavy weight in the back. It was fun.

In about late March, I started looking for a job. I ended up getting a job at Bartlett Tree Experts and put in seven months with them. I've been very fortunate. I had some good mentors along the way. I had one guy who told me, "Remember, Michael, you don't want to be the world's fastest tree climber. You want to be the world's oldest."

Michael Biddy, 2021

I made it through seven months [with Bartlett]. At the time there was an epidemic of dead elm trees, and you could find elm trees to cut down just by driving around, knocking on doors. Everybody needed an elm tree cut down. I was a little bit wild, at that point — nobody's gonna take that kind of job if they're sane. But that was the beginning of my business. This is my 51st year. I'm picking my spots now, but I'm still doing it. I got all this cool equipment now.

I go way back with the Blue Benn. I remember pre-Sonny. The coffee was awful. And the service was not very elegant or friendly. The food, to put it plainly, was sub-par and that's being polite. I probably went in there once and didn't go back.

I wouldn't have called it a dive, just a non-inspiring diner in a beautiful building. When Sonny and Mary Lou took over, she did a lot of spiffing up over the years. She made it feel cleaner and more diner-like. Word of mouth spread pretty fast. I must have heard talk that you could get a good meal there with the new owners.

Sonny was just a very imaginative cook. I remember when he started cooking Mexican food — back in the eighties — enchilada platters and stuff. He came up with a killer omelet, a California omelet, that I was in love with ... with sour cream and avocados and sprouts and cheese. That omelet was — wow! I mean, avocados were on it. The seventies? In Vermont? And about that time, Sonny started making bouillabaisse soup. He used all kinds of different sea-food in it. He'd offer it once a week and that was worth scheduling. He really was adventurous.

I'm gonna go aside here a bit. I did a lot of tree work for them at their home, as well. And I used to decorate — for Mary Lou, I used to decorate a couple really tall spruce trees. This is in the eighties. But before that, I did a lot of tree work at their house as well, with ropes, before I had a bucket truck. At one point I got a tour of the house, including the basement. Now this is where my perspective on Sonny is different from other people, after what I saw in the basement.

Sonny had a row of tall, deep filing cabinets, absolutely filled with recipes. He was a recipe junkie. He loved to collect recipes and research them. They were like his library. And I got to see his basement in the home, with at least two, four-drawer — deep drawer — filing cabinets full of recipes.

I'm definitely a food looker. That was a big thing in the Blue Benn. A plate would come out and you'd catch people eyeing it. Then they'd say, "Mmm, what is that?" [*laughs*] It was a good way to start a conversation with a stranger. Most people would go into the diner swimming in ideas of "What am I gonna eat?" Then you see one of those plates come out of the kitchen, and you go, "Ah, that's what I want."

The Blue Benn waitresses had their own way of catering to the regulars. There wasn't a lot of honey this and sweetie that; it wasn't like your typical kind of diner banter. But the waitresses became, in effect, your friends. They were your agents, your representatives between the kitchen and your plate. It was the little things, like Sonny's sister Pat telling me, "Don't let them butter your toast in the kitchen; I'll butter it for you out here, because we have butter out here, and they use margarine in the kitchen."

They became your diner buddies, in a way. They knew what you wanted. If I ordered buckwheat pancakes, they'd say, "What's the matter? No blueberries today?" They would talk to you about people that you knew and that weren't there. It was always good; they weren't dishing the dirt or anything, just sharing news.

One day Sharon was talking with me. She leaned across the counter, her elbows on the glass-topped container where they kept the silverware and napkins and stuff. I guess she wanted to tell an important detail with a bit more privacy, so she leaned in closer and —CRASH — the top shatters under her elbows. [*laughs*] Everyone starts laughing and someone's shouting "Where's Sharon? That had to be Sharon." She had a bit of a reputation for dropping stuff. [*laughs*]

Diners are tricky, because everybody that works there has to get along with everybody else, or else it's not gonna work. Obviously, there are always going to be tensions between people. But it becomes like a family. It was like family.

I've been missing it since it closed.* I've been missing all those things we talked about, the food, the familiarity and the friendliness. All of it. It was like an extended family.

** Michael spoke at the height of the pandemic — masked and socially distant — when lockdown restrictions were still in place.*

I met a woman whose eyes were tired
She sat down next to me in a diner
She was talking about the better days
When everybody she knew could get their bills paid
But now the times have changed around her
Forgotten factories surround her
— From "Her Escape" by Erik Bovino

Lisa LaFlamme and Erik Bovino

Erik Bovino

The Younger Generation

The first time Erik Bovino visited Sonny's Blue Benn Diner was to eat. After a 45-minute wait for one of the six coveted booths, Erik and his teammates — all rowers at Williams College — ordered more food than they could fit on the table. The second visit was for homework. Assigned a research project in sociology, Erik spent three months interviewing staff and customers at the diner. The experience, he says, would change his life, inspiring him to quit college and spend two years writing and performing his own music. It was the stories he heard and the lives he encountered that coaxed a creative turning point in his life. Erik is currently a senior at Vanderbilt University and recently released an album under the stage name Erik Mason. One song on the album, Her Escape, came out of his many talks with Lisa Monroe.

How did the Blue Benn become an assignment? What was the class and why did you choose the Benn?

The class was an ethnographic research class, which is a very open-ended kind of word, depending on how you interpret it. Basically, the assignment was to find a group of people or a certain niche population in some way and get to know them and understand their story and tell their story and explain what was going on in that population, what defined them and united them.

The project was to run over the course of the semester. We had to go do interviews and observational reporting. Some of my friends went to the local veterans' organization. Some went to some drug rehab facilities and started talking with people who were in rehab. Stuff like that. I got a little more creative. Luckily, the professor was on board with the idea.

I always loved diners — I'm from New Jersey, and diners are a really big thing there. I grew up going to one down the street from me, and my friends and I would go to one after practices and musicals, near where I went to school in New Jersey. So I had an attachment to diners and the experience of going there with friends and getting diner food.

So how many visits did you make to the diner?

In total, I think it was maybe five or six, maximum.

Because it seems like you got a good feel for the place, even after that amount of time.

Well, yeah. I spent hours there, on some days. Like the interview with Lisa was around three hours. A couple days I showed up at the wrong time and ended up just hanging out, waiting for her to come. and I'd end up interviewing the other waitresses and just observing. I feel as if it's such a small place, that once you start talking to people, you get to know it.

I wonder in being there, if you walked away with a sense of the community, of the people that ate there, of the Bennington-ness of it?

One of the things that struck me is that there were so many different people with different backgrounds.

You have truck drivers who come in before their journey down the interstate or teachers coming in for breakfast before heading to the local elementary school or wealthier families who retired in the area. And they all come there because they know how good the food is. But even more important than that, and I think this is really interesting, it's a place where everyone can go and leave their status on the doorstep, before they come in.

That's a really interesting observation. Looking at it from a sociological point of view, did it seem to have a leveling effect on anyone who walked in?

Absolutely. In sociology we do study the characteristics that unite people of different statuses or social classes, so I was really curious to see how that might be reflected in a diner setting.

"It's a very egalitarian place,"

Everyone's sitting in the same area, and it's so small you can overhear conversations, and for an hour of your day, you're just surrounded by people who may be very different, but are all there together. It's a very egalitarian place.

There's a book written by the sociologist Ray Oldenburg about what he calls the "third place." It's not home, it's not work, it's a community place that's by its nature inclusive. It draws people in and, in that sense, helps really bind the community together.

Exactly. There was definitely a community aspect to it. I would hear stories of people who would come in weekly, at the same time every day. The waitresses would recognize people who walked in, who hadn't been there for months and they'd get into a conversation.

I think the community aspect of the diner was tied to the staff, their warmth and their empathy. I think people who came in responded to that. The atmosphere of the place nurtured a sense of community, for sure.

It seems like what you observed up to a point was that the staff was a cohesive unit. They were fantastic with the customers and all worked together; but I wonder whether you left with that impression.

The diner experience isn't performative in any way. They don't put on a show, when you're there. It comes about naturally — people who enjoy doing their job and feel proud of the food they're serving. It's not some Disneyland experience, like you walk into one of the diners on Main Street, USA, that's completely fabricated. It's not that at all in the Blue Benn. The people who worked at the diner were genuine.

At the end of the day, it fell on Lisa to make sure things were running smoothly, and people were getting paid, and bills were getting paid. Everyone else could just go home and leave their stresses from the workplace at the workplace. ... Lisa being an only child and having the diner in her life from such a young age, that put her in a very unique position. I think my general conclusion at the end of the paper is that, yes, this diner "experience" is a real thing; but when you're the one running the show, it's different — you're not really part of the experience you create, you're just trying to get mouths fed and the bills paid.

Lisa especially seemed to have a big impact on you.

She inspired the song *Her Escape*. I had never written a song like that before, where it was deeply personal and about people who I couldn't really relate to, whose lives

Jessica Gardner and Kim Corey

were so different from my own. It was the combination of the paper and my experiences at the Benn that made me want to explore the stories of others and put those into music.

Is it fair to say that the series of interviews you conducted at the Blue Benn pushed you to examine your own life more than you might have otherwise living in the ultimate college bubble?

I know I come from a place of privilege in society. But I think that the contrast was just so sharp, going from Williams to the Benn and back to Williams. They're two completely different social spaces, social environments. That's what really stood out to me.

Again, it wasn't like I walked into the Benn and I had a revelation about inequality in the world. But the interviews I had with the customers and the staff definitely was like, damn, this is a real thing. You don't just hear it in music, this goes on in the lives of people across the country. And as a 19-year-old student in an elite college, you're not often exposed to that kind of stuff. I was on such a different path at that point, and hearing the stories of others, who didn't share my luck and the chance to be whoever they wanted to be was — it was disheartening. I felt compelled to share that sort of feeling and reality with the rest of the world, through my music.

So you decided to drop out and pursue a record deal?

Yeah, that was when I sort of decided I wanted to take time off from school. At that point I'd only written three songs, one of which was an incomplete version of *Her Escape*, and to me, that was enough to say, all right, there's more I want to say. Let's take some time and just focus on this.

Record deal? No. It was basically an independent venture. I booked my own shows, and I tried to get my music out there as much as I could. It's tough, as an independent musician, especially having no experience. But when I was living in New York, I'd play at the Bitter End, I played at Pianos, which is another bar that's well known. I ended up moving back to New Jersey, living in Asbury Park, where there's a very big music scene of local artists. I've played at the Stone Pony, which is very well known — an old Springsteen hangout.

One more question, what did you get on the paper?

[*Laughs*] I think he gave me an A. I remember him saying it was a little "sappy," but then he said, "We want to post this on the sociology website," as a sample paper type. That was good.

CD cover: Erik Bovino recording as Erik Mason
Courtesy Erik Bovino

BREAKFAST IN SILK CITY

Sonny's Blue Benn and the Dichotomy of the "Diner Experience"

This is an excerpt from Eric Bovino's 2017 paper written for Anthropology & Sociology 205, Ways of Knowing, at Williams College.

It was a frigid January morning when my four friends and I departed our dormitories at Williams College, eager to satisfy appetites that had grown large from the toil of a Saturday morning rowing practice. Crammed into a Subaru Outback, we pulled out of the parking lot and headed up the winding tarmac of Route 7. We were in search of a renowned eatery about 25 minutes north in Bennington, Vermont, known throughout the college for it delicious menu, huge portions and nostalgic vibe.

... I have come to understand that the operation of the Blue Benn is not as idyllic as the experience a customer has when he or she eats there. Behind the warm service, nostalgic atmosphere and tasty food exists one man's vision. Now, the second generation of family is struggling to keep his Silk City dream alive.

... It was [my parents] "good cop, bad cop chemistry" that made the operation run so smoothly, remembers Lisa [LaFlamme], who was just 10 years old when the Blue Benn entered her life. "Dad didn't like to deal with things. He just loved working in the kitchen and he wanted everything to run smoothly."

... Her mother enjoyed her own responsibilities just as much — interacting with customers, handling finances and maintenance, and being the smiling face that ushered newcomers to their tables. It was a winning formula that in the coming years would resurrect the ramshackle railcar into a regional icon.

... That the Blue Benn treats all of their customers equally, from the blue-collared local to the Tony-winning actress, is very significant in the completion of the diner experience as a whole. It creates a sense of consistency for all customers that, regardless of status, every person will be put on a level playing field.

... Sonny and Mary Lou made sure the Blue Benn served as a safety net for any family member in need. In many respects, the Blue Benn became a family business as much by chance as it did on purpose. Although Sonny and Mary Lou intended for their daughter to be a contributing member of the operation, economic changes brought [extended] family even closer than they could've predicted. They've watched each other become mothers and grandmothers and great aunts over the decades of working in the confines of the diner. Perhaps this explains the warmth and welcome-ness that is so present in the Blue Benn; it is a space illuminated by the comfort and ease of being with family.

Zoë Sperber & Gabrielle Mele-Algus

The Younger Generation

Zoë and Gabrielle don't remember the first time they met — at toddler playgroup — but they have no doubt the connection was immediate. As little girls they begged their mothers to buy them matching outfits. In high school they kept each other's teenage secrets, confiding about boys and school and dreams of life beyond Bennington. Not long out of college the two shared an apartment in Boston, meeting up again after adventuring into the wider world. It was a time in their lives when both had begun to recognize the value of their small-town roots, of growing up in a place where they felt nurtured by more than just their families, but by a community of friends and neighbors as well. "Growing up in a small town grounds you. You feel part of community and that can be tremendously supportive," says Zoë. For Gabs, "the Blue Benn was a part of that sense of community."

Gabs: I moved here from New Jersey when I was nine months old.

Zoë: And joined the baby group. We're three months apart so I must have been about a year old.

Gabs: We were together until kindergarten. And then

Blue Benn menu, pre-Sonny and Mary Lou

we went to different elementary and middle schools. And then we were back together in high school.

Zoë: But we still saw each other all the time, during that time, even though we weren't in the same schools. Gabs lives in Shaftsbury, and I went to Benn El and then got homeschooled. [*laughs*] Actually, when I got homeschooled, Gabrielle was super jealous because I got to go to the Blue Benn all the time. [*laughs*]

Gabs: Every day for lunch, she went to the Blue Benn.

Zoë: Not every day. In Gab's mind, we went every single day. No, some days we'd meet my dad at the Benn for lunch. After high school, I went to Smith. I took my junior year in Santiago, Chile, and after I graduated, I lived there for another two years. I came home, and moved in with Gabs, in Somerville [Massachusetts]. I lived there for two years and then I went off to law school — sadly, had to leave my dear roommate. [*laughs*]

Gabs: I went to Brown for college and then to Tufts for grad school for occupational therapy. So that's why I was living in Somerville, where we lived together. By the time Zoë moved in, I'd already done two years of grad school, and had studied in Sweden for a semester. When I got back from Sweden, Zoë moved in with me. Because of the pandemic I came home from March 13 until June 21. I was only coming home for a weekend and ended up staying three months. [*laughs*]

When I came home recently, I found a timeline I'd made as a teenager. Under "Two Years Old" it said birthday party at Blue Benn. I don't remember that but I do remember that growing up, our family went to the diner once or twice a week every week.

Zoë: I know that Pat [Sheppard] knew us from when we were really little, because she would always do cute things for us.

Gabs: Yeah, we used to get an extra whipped cream.

Zoë: We'd order hot chocolate, and it came with whipped cream. Pat just started giving us extra cream and then she'd give us a mug — you know, those skinny, diner coffee mugs — just filled with whipped cream. As we got older, she'd just put the whipped cream container on the counter. Our parents would sit in a booth and we'd be up to no good at the counter with the whipped cream. [*laughs*]

Gabs: If they were near the end of a whipped cream container, she'd would just give it to us. She'd just leave it and we'd Reddi-Wip away. [*laughs*]

Zoë: Oh, yeah. I'm sure our parents really appreciated that.

Gabs: You would eat the stuff off the top and then slather another layer on top.

Zoë: Always [*laughing*].

Gabs: When we were little, we sat at the counter most of the time. We'd usually try to sit where there was a jukebox. The jukeboxes [at the counter] are spaced out and some had a reputation for breaking down.

Zoë: When you walk in the door, over on the far left, in the corner there — that's prime spot, next to the coatrack, because it had a jukebox right there.

Gabs: It was also definitely the spot where we could heckle the waitresses. And we would, a lot. [*laughs*] I remember one time, when you got an expandable fork — where'd you get that?

Zoë: Oh, I loved that thing.

Gabs: Sharon was our waitress, and Zoë and I kept trying to expand her fork to make the soda machine go. I don't think we got it, but I just remember trying.

Zoë: The waitresses were always so nice. They thought we were funny. I don't think they cared. They knew that we were good kids; we weren't gonna ruin one of their pies or something.

By the time we got to high school we were almost protective of the waitresses. [*laughs*]

Gabs: Because we grew up going there all the time, we really respected the staff. So if I was going there with friends, I was like, "Guys, we can't try and have more than four of us in this booth; maybe we can fit a fifth, but we can't put a chair in the aisle, because that annoys the waitresses."

Zoë: The thing about the Blue Benn is that it was such a comfortable spot for the locals. You could order what you loved and expected it to be the same every time, and it was.

Although I remember one time [*laughing*] I was there with my parents and they ordered the clam chowder as a starter. Either Heidi or Sharon, I don't remember which one, was like, "You don't want to order that today. It's very thick. We ran out of milk. It's too thick. We can't thin it." And whoever it was, one of my parents was like, "Oh, it's fine. Just bring it out." And she brought it out and stuck the spoon —really dramatically, in the middle of the bowl, and it just stood up straight.

But apart from that one weird time, I'd usually get soup. I loved their soup.

Gabs: Or maybe grilled cheese? Chicken tenders? I had a period that I really loved their chicken tenders. And their sweet potato fries — so good.

Zoë: So good. I also used to get the grilled Turkey Mesa sandwich. Ooh, that was good. It had spicy mayo on it and they'd put them on the grill — the bread was just saturated in butter — and it'd get really crispy on the top.

Gabs: It was where you'd bring friends when they came home with you from college — even now, if I bring friends there when I'm visiting. It's a staple, when I'm home, to go there. If I do come home for a weekend and don't eat there, I'm always like, "Hey, I didn't get to go to the Blue Benn this weekend."

Zoë: [*Laughing*] "I didn't get to overstuff myself into oblivion at the Blue Benn."

To me the diner was one of the few authentically Bennington experiences left in town. It's not fancy, which is one reason why local people like it, and it has creative and interesting food.

Gabs: And it was always there, no matter what.

Zoë: Everything changed around it, except the diner.

Growing up here you realize there's a lot about Bennington that is kind of sad — like the fact that so many things have come and gone, or that for a long time the local businesses downtown were dying out. But the Blue Benn was the one constant. You knew you could bring somebody there, and that it's gonna be good. It'll also be a very small-town, comfy experience, that the waitresses would all know me and always ask questions about my life or my family — "Oh, your mom told me . . ." whatever.

Gabs: That's the thing; when you're at college, you

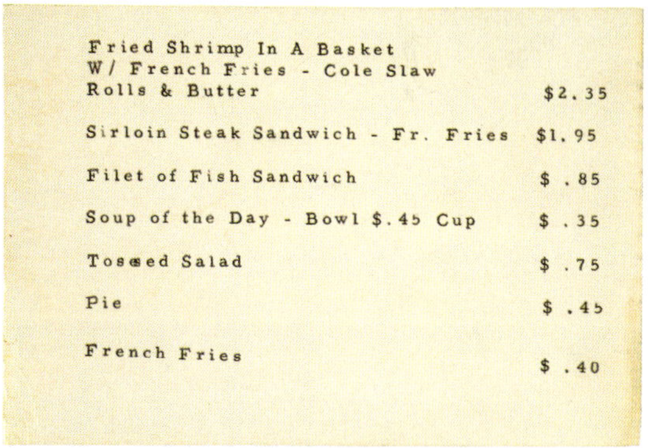

Fried Shrimp In A Basket W/ French Fries - Cole Slaw Rolls & Butter	$2.35
Sirloin Steak Sandwich - Fr. Fries	$1.95
Filet of Fish Sandwich	$ .85
Soup of the Day - Bowl $.45 Cup	$ .35
Tossed Salad	$ .75
Pie	$ .45
French Fries	$ .40

Blue Benn menu, circa 1975, by Sonny and Mary Lou

Family and staff

can glorify your hometown however much you want, and then you bring friends home, and you're like, "There's this diner, we have to go" — who knows what they're thinking? They're probably like, "Is she making this up? Does everybody really know everybody? How small town is this place?" And then you walk in, and the waitresses are, like, "Hey, Gabs! How's it going? How's college?" And they know everything.

Zoë: It's just fun, because when you're from a tiny town, and your peers are from New York City or whatever, and you're just like, "Yeah, I'm from Bennington, Vermont, … so you have to make it the best of where you come from.Maybe you've got Chinese takeout till 5:00 a.m., but the waitresses here know me and give me free whipped cream."

Their reaction? "My god, this is so small-town." [*laughs*]

Gabs: Or, "How does this person know so much about you?"

But I think it was that the sense of home that really made the Blue Benn special. You'd walk in and the waitresses would say, "Oh, your mom told me that. …" So you're bringing friends there to see the place or you're there to catch up with old friends, but you're also catching up with the waitresses and most of all, your catching up with your hometown.

Jeff Yucht

A Mix Of Regulars

In the late 1980s, Jeff Yucht was working as an emergency room doctor in Detroit, "a crazy gun and knife club," as he puts it. He tells the story of an addict on the run from the cops who, desperate to conceal evidence, downed a hefty packet of heroin. Using a tube with the girth of a garden hose to pump his stomach, Jeff managed to save the man's life. "He looks at me, with my Doc Yucht, Detroit Receiving Hospital nametag, and says, 'Dr. Yucht, you tell the cops about this, I will kill you.' In that moment, I realized that I just didn't want to do emergency medicine in a city," says Jeff of the decision that brought him to Vermont. "I wish I could say it was just the Blue Benn, but I fell in love with Bennington," he laughs. Dr. Yucht has practiced emergency medicine at Southwestern Vermont Medical Center ever since.

I think of the Blue Benn as the family practice of restaurants. In family practice, you deliver the kids and you see those same kids grow up. For me, the Blue Benn waitresses had a family-practice relationship with their customers. They made the diner special. The same staff were there, decade after decade. You got to know them, and they got to know you, your wife and your kids.

Rob [Sperber] and I would go out to lunch all the time. I've been working here for decades, and we basi-

"Brian and Sonny are working. ... I mean, it's crazy. It's like nothing is gonna stop those two. I'm standing there, sewing up a hand, and doing this at the sink, and these guys are like, 'It's a normal day at the Blue Benn.'"

— Jeff Yucht

cally have been doing lunch for literally 20 years, going to different places in town, including many places that have come and gone. In those other places, the staff would be friendly and they'd know you, but it wasn't the same. I mean, Sharon had been working at the diner for 30 years! And Heidi, what, almost 25 years? No restaurant keeps people for 25 years or 40 years, in Pat's case. It just doesn't happen. They knew our sons [Miles and Leo] and watched them grow up. Jeannie remembered Leo coming in for hot chocolate as a little kid, now he's 26. To this day Leo talks about how Jeannie would put extra whipped cream in his hot chocolate. To this day, no hot chocolate's good enough for Leo, because no place puts that much whipped cream in it. That experience, that connection is hard to duplicate. It's what made the diner so special.

I'd say Sharon's version of the kitchen operation was pretty accurate, but here's what I remember: So Rob and I are having lunch. What were we eating? It is funny, there's a handful of things that we always ate — probably about seven or eight things that were sort of the standards for us. I wish I could remember what I ate that day, but I'll just say the usual. [*laughs*] [See the interview with Sharon Gavin on page 63 for the waitress's version of the story.]

Sharon comes out and, yeah, she was wearing some kind of glove, but the blood was seeping though and it was obvious she'd cut herself. Badly. I must have said, "You better get it taken care of," and she said no. She wasn't gonna go to the ER. I can't remember if she had insurance or if she didn't have insurance. I think that may have been one of the reasons why she didn't want to go, or maybe the deductible was too high. But she was adamant — "I don't want to go. I gotta work. I have things to do." And the girls were on her case too, the rest of the waitresses. They're all like, "You gotta get this taken care of."

Sharon has diabetes and — you have to take care of her. You can't do nothing. It wasn't a terrible cut, but clearly needed a couple of stitches. She just wanted to work. She was like, "I gotta work." So I said, "Well, let's do it here." But I had to go over to the hospital to get things. As a matter of fact, I think Robbie was the one that said, "Ah, Jeff, just go and come back." I think Rob was the one who volunteered my services, really put me in a … [*laughs*]

So I went back to the hospital, picked up the standard things you would need to suture and came back to the diner. This is completely illegal. Actually, if you came to me 10 years ago, and asked me to tell this story I'd would have said no. But I'm now, I'm near the end of my career. My job is more fun, these days. I work very little — seven days a month and I get to read a bunch and keep up, and I don't have to worry about medicine becoming so rules-based.

So, when you say, "Is it legal?" Eh, you know, no. But I don't care. My feeling is, it was the right thing to do, to help her. Sometimes, rules, as you know, take on a life of their own. And sometimes we just, we blindly follow them for no particular reason. I've always practiced medicine on the premise that my responsibility is to the patient.

When I got back from the hospital, Sharon was still working, with the glove on. She doesn't stop. She's a machine. We went back into the kitchen; the parking lot wasn't an option. And I gotta tell you, that kitchen is small. And there's not a flat surface to work on. I don't remember what we used for light, but I do remember we did it right by the sink. One of the keys is irrigating stuff, the wound, so the sink was handy. She's holding out her hand — look, for me, sewing someone or doing suturing is so minor. But I can see how it might have been a little nerve-wracking for her. [*laughs*] …

Meantime, Brian and Sonny are working. They're doing orders. I mean, it's crazy. It's like nothing is gonna stop those two. I'm standing there, sewing up a hand, and doing this at the sink, and these guys are like, "It's a normal day at the Blue Benn."

Really, if there was any humor in it, that was it, how no one batted an eyelash. They didn't even slow down. These guys are going at 100 miles an hour all the time. They had their system [*snapping fingers*] and nothing stopped them.

It was phenomenal. The place worked like a well-oiled machine.

"Breafast at the Blue Benn Diner,"
audiotape by Tom Weakley, 2001

Bob & Cora Howe

A Mix Of Regulars

Bob and Cora Howe's living room is spacious and warm, made up of things crafted by Bob and collected by Cora. There's a tumble of books spread out over one end of the couch and more cascading from a nearby bookshelf. The place makes clear that whoever lives here is intensely curious about the world and the way it works. At 88 and 87 years old, Bob and Cora have been together for 70 years, marrying as high school sweethearts. Their journey together has been remarkable, seemingly encompassing several lifetimes. Bob has been a teacher, a craftsman, an inventor and an entrepreneur. Cora raised the couple's four children and worked alongside Bob, helping him steer through the curves of his swerving career path. Theirs is a quintessential Vermont story.

Cora: Bob was always restless.

Bob: I taught shop for 12 years in Bennington, but I felt like I wasn't in the world enough. The two of us were so young that we didn't have a chance to do things young people do. We were parents of babies and we were babies ourselves.

Cora: Well, you went off to college several times. Bob ended up getting four or five degrees and I kept packing up and moving our family.

Bob: When our kids were at the Prospect School in North Bennington, that's where I met David Kelso [in about 1971]. He was teaching there. He's an unbelievable, creative, crazy guy.

Cora: Well, he asked you if you could help him out with an idea, because he knew that you were so great with your hands.

Bob: So we invented a backpack, and we put the heavy tape recorder on the back, and then we made this arm that comes up around like this [*swinging his arm in an arc*], with a shelf on it so you could put a camera on it. That's the Porta-Brace. That's where the Porta-Brace company name came from. ... We ran the company for 32 years. We morphed into making cases, soft cases for cameras and recorders.

Cora: Bob ran the company. I did a very hands-on, on-the-floor job there. I was the quality control person. Bob did all the management and the design and everything else, but I got along very well with the employees. Bob did too, they adored him. ... Everything grew gradually, because we weren't gonna get ourselves in terribly big debt.

Bob: It was tough going for a while. We didn't really have the money to go out.

Cora: No, we never went out at all. When our kids were little, it was a huge event to go out.

We started going to the Blue Benn, probably when I started working more full-time at Porta-Brace. Probably the mid-seventies. It was when Lisa, Sonny and Mary Lou's daughter, was little. You know [*laughs*] you get as old as we are, and you lose track of how many years.

Bob: I think we probably went there most of the —

whenever we ate out, that's where we went. For a long time it was like that. It was our type of place. Down-home. A family place.

Cora: Exactly. It was very inexpensive and very welcoming. Cozy and comfortable and it was a place we could afford; great food — you got certainly the best breakfast anywhere around.

Bob: I loved the quesadillas.

Cora: Not me. That's not my thing. I'm more inclined to — well, the vegetable omelet that they do, for instance, that's delicious. I like that a lot. Soup — the soups are wonderful.

Bob: Oh yeah, I used to love the gazpacho soup.

Cora: Lisa, their daughter, was around the diner a lot from the time she was little. On Friday evenings, she'd be there, maybe because the next day wasn't a school day. I remember one time, when she was maybe 10 years old, maybe younger, she'd greet you as you came in the door. I'm not sure if it was just people she knew or everyone, but she'd welcome you and take you to your seat. [*laughs*] She was like a little cruise director on a passenger ship, like *The Love Boat*, which was on TV at the time. It was her little game and it was so sweet. It was just lovely.

Bob: One of the things I remember was at various times seeing customers buying a meal for some old guy who clearly had no money.

Cora: I think that wasn't overt. Nobody was trying to make any show of it. But there are a few people, from time to time, who'd come in, who obviously are very poor, very poorly off. Older men have been the ones that I've noticed. And they give them — the waitresses would — free food.

Bob: And some of the customers, also, will give them — pay for their meal. We've seen that done.

Cora: It's done sweetly, quietly; nobody has to feel any shame. The Blue Benn was the kind of place where anyone could walk through the door and feel comfortable. And we've more than once asked somebody else what they were eating, or people have asked us, because it looked good, what they were getting. And that's perfectly OK.

Bob: It didn't diminish the atmosphere, but there was always a hard-and-fast rule at the diner, and they don't have any tolerance for breaking the rule, that if anybody just walks in and sits at the counter and then tries to move to a table, they're out. You had to wait for a booth, no matter who you were. There was something sort of democratic about that rule. And there's something about sitting out in the vestibule, sitting there waiting with other people. Sometimes you don't say anything, sometimes you really talk it up with people. I think it helped break down barriers between people.

"You had to wait for a booth, no matter who you were."

Cora: But I think for anyone in Bennington, doesn't matter who you are, I think they all are willing to go in the Blue Benn — if they can get in. That was the biggest thing, is getting in, because they were so busy all the time.

Bob: There was a time when Rob [Sperber] and I went to the diner every week. It was a standing thing on Saturday mornings and I paid for the breakfast. [*laughs*] That's because I was over at his shop quite a lot — he was kind of my woodworking mentor. We just talked

The entryway sign: STOP If you would like a booth, we will let you know when one becomes available. If there are open spots at the counter, please help yourself!

Opposite: Cleveland Plain Dealer, Sept. 14, 2014

about woodworking and all the stuff that he does. He's a machinist and — you know, he's way, way beyond me.

Cora: Oh, stop.

Bob: Well, he is.

Rob Sperber tells a somewhat different version. Both had graduated from the Rochester Institute of Technology 20 years apart and are both inventors and craftsmen. There was plenty of talk about machines and woodworking at those Saturday meetings, but Rob remembers thoughtful discussions about business as well. "Bob made me realize that business doesn't have to be cutthroat and that your employees should feel that they're a respected part of the team," he says.

Bob: The reason we created Porta-Brace was for people to have a good place to work and make a living. We weren't in the business of trying to make a lot of money and I think that's one of the reasons it was so successful.

Their businesses couldn't be more different, but Bob and Cora and Sonny and Mary Lou shared a work ethic that included treating their employees with respect and kindness. Their staff, at Porta-Brace and Sonny's Blue Benn, paid them back with loyalty rarely seen.

Bob: We weren't in the business of trying to make a lot of money. We just wanted to make a good place to work. That was the philosophy. And when people came in and worked for us, they loved it.

I remember talking to Sonny once, suggesting he expand the business and he said no, no they wanted to stay the way they were. I understood that. We'd had a lot of people —Panasonic for one — asking us to go bigger. But like Sonny we were more interested in keeping the business a good place to work than taking it to another level.

Visiting Vermont | The Food

JOE CREA | CLEVLAND.COM

Dozens of daily specials line the walls of the Blue Benn Diner, a dining institution in Bennington, Vermont.

On the road, places for fine dining, homestyle grub and gourmet to-go

RUBBER DUCKY

The Blue Benn's jukebox has long evoked strong feelings, as evidenced by a note two patrons left behind on a napkin.

As a long-time lover of the Blue Benn and all it represents, I have a vested interest in maintaining the quality and personality of the Blue Benn breakfast experience. When the Blue Benn shifted from the 1962 jukebox to the Silver City a lamentable omission occurred: *Rubber Ducky* (the beloved children's classic) was not included in the new collection. Over the years, *Rubber Ducky* has come to symbolize the Blue Benn. I looked forward to blueberry pancakes, a counter seat with my Dad, and Ernie's heartfelt homage to America's favorite bath toy. Today, the silence in the Blue Benn is deafening. It is not so much a tragedy for me, as it is a travesty for the next generation of Blue Benners. *Rubber Ducky* is a part of the Blue Benn; it is a part of my childhood; it is a part of who I am. It is vital to the heritage — the continuity — of this establishment. *Rubber Ducky* is more than a song. It is the anthem of the working people and their children. It is the battle cry of small-town family values. When the Blue Benn surrendered that song it surrendered its connection to the people. Bring back *Rubber Ducky.* Bring it back for the children, but most importantly, bring back *Rubber Ducky* for yourselves.

Sincerely,
Karin Colgan,
South Londonderry, Vt.
Joanna Rucco,
Sandgate, Vt.

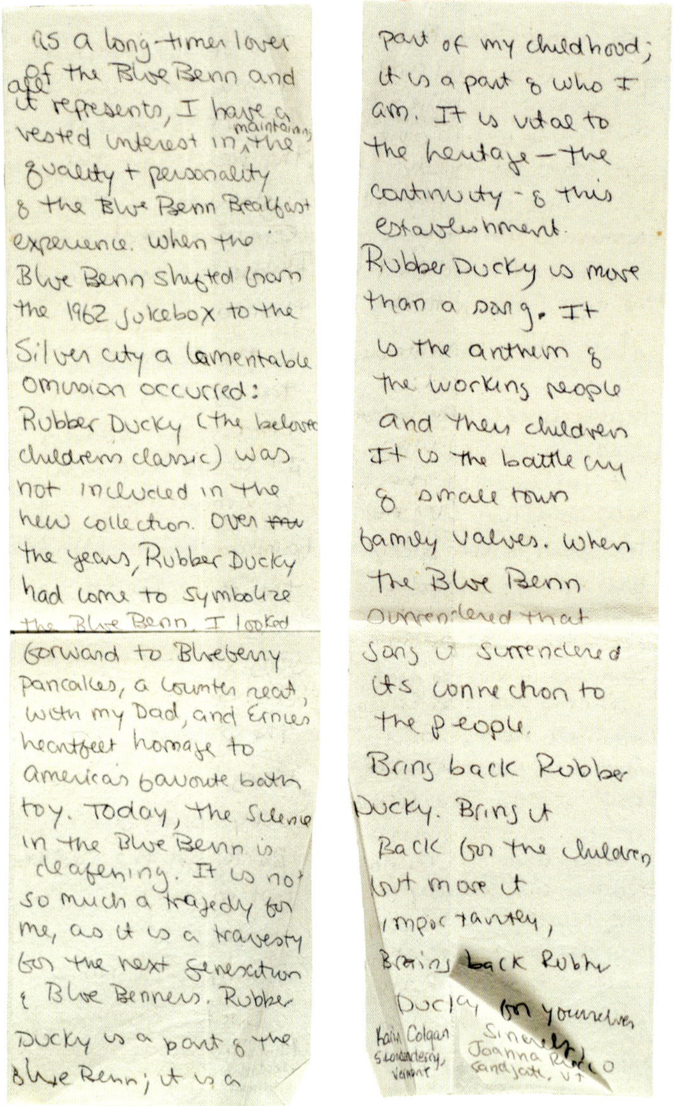

as a long-time lover of the Blue Benn and all it represents, I have a vested interest in maintaining the quality + personality of the Blue Benn Breakfast experience. When the Blue Benn shifted from the 1962 jukebox to the Silver City a lamentable omission occurred: Rubber Ducky (the beloved childrens classic) was not included in the new collection. Over the years, Rubber Ducky had come to symbolize the Blue Benn. I looked forward to Blueberry pancakes, a counter seat, with my Dad, and Ernies heartfeet homage to America's favorite bath toy. Today, the silence in the Blue Benn is deafening. It is not so much a tragedy for me, as it is a travesty for the next generation of Blue Benners. Rubber Ducky is a part of the Blue Benn; it is a part of my childhood; it is a part of who I am. It is vital to the heritage – the continuity of this establishment. Rubber Ducky is more than a song. It is the anthem of the working people and their children It is the battle cry of small town family values. When the Blue Benn surrendered that song it surrendered its connection to the people. Bring back Rubber Ducky. Bring it back for the children but more importantly, Bring back Rubber Ducky for yourselves

Sincerely
Karin Colgan
S. Londonderry, Vermont
Joanna Rucco
Sandgate, VT

Jim Woodward

A Mix Of Regulars

Jim Woodward is musing about old times, back in the 1980s when Bennington College was tagged "the most decadent college in America" and a hotbed of free spirits. "Oh my Lord, the 'Dress to Get Laid' parties were national news. It was like something out of the Dadaist movement … with the most outrageous outfits, little metal things covering just enough." It was also a time when the college launched a string of extraordinary young writers, including Donna Tartt, Bret Easton Ellis and Jonathan Lethem. "I liked the wildness and the crazy, it felt like anything could happen and that fed into the creativity," Jim says, adding that it was in those years that the students emerged from their magical kingdom to mingle with the "townies" in places like Sonny's Blue Benn and the Carousel Club where James was a DJ. "It was a time when there was a lot of interplay between the townspeople and the students. None of the exclusivity you see today. … There were no boundaries in those days."

I am 60 — I have to stop and think about it. Isn't that weird? I am 67. I was born here in the fifties, the early fifties, went to high school here, moved to New York as an 18-year-old. I tried that out and got steamrollered. It seemed like everything that I wanted to see and do there, I could do better as a tourist than as a

Cheryl Gilman

resident. Then I went to art school — the Art Institute in Boston. I lived there for several years after school, got involved in the club scene and was enthralled with the music scene.

On one of my trips back to Bennington, I heard that they were opening a nightclub nearby. I got a job DJ-ing the music and moved back here. The club was called Carousel, right on the New York border. I started there in '74, maybe, and stayed to around '84. It was a real crazy place for many years and then it burned to the ground after a new owner took over. After that I worked anyplace that had electricity and an electrical outlet.

"For me it feels like the Blue Benn has always been there, a part of Bennington."

I always had a second job, but that music was the thing that I did and loved, and still do, believe it or not. Can't hear out of either ear, but I still do it. Basically now I just do special events; lot of weddings, lot of parties. I used to do promotion events for the town.

For me it feels like the Blue Benn has always been there, a part of Bennington. It's kind of like wallpaper: you don't always notice it there, but you know when it's gone. And the Monroes didn't take it over until — Jesus. There were several other people beforehand.

But it wasn't a *thing* back then, it was just like any of several other diners in town. It wasn't really anything different or special. If you had to put a time or date on when it shifted, it'd probably be after Sonny and Mary Lou bought it. Slowly but surely it became a meeting spot. The food was good; the integrity of Sonny's food was always really great — you knew what you were gonna get, and it didn't vary. The Blue Benn hit all the right boxes. It appealed to everyone, whether you were high-end, New York City, or from over-the-tracks in Pownal, whatever.

When you'd walk into the place there would always be theme music playing. Everybody was totally fascinated by the little jukebox things and everybody used to ask, "Do these actually work?" Well, they did. People would come in with kids, and it would be like showing them how to use a rotary phone. They had no idea what a "45" is, much less a jukebox. There was always music going and certain songs that you'd hear over and over again — we'd have to hear "Rubber Ducky," by the Muppets, which I could've lived without, and of course "Moonlight in Vermont." Patsy Cline's "Crazy" was a big one and Elvis. Toward the end, they actually put in more contemporary stuff, which for me as a music guy was nice.

I knew Sonny, but he was an early-morning guy, he'd be in the kitchen at dawn baking pies or cooking and unless you got there early-early, you didn't have any interaction with him. I was a Sunday brunch kind of guy. I'd be there on a Sunday, and I'd order a hangover breakfast — huevos rancheros or sausage biscuits. Well, you'd get a side of Heidi, too, because she just has no filter. She was sassy, which was part of the charm of the waitresses there. She'd know what I did the night before and be telling me what I should have for breakfast for my hangover. [*laughs*]

I'm very happy that the guy who bought the Blue Benn [John Getchell] really wants to keep the integrity of the place. I met [John] at Bennington College in the early eighties. He was part of a whole crew there at that time,

Jim Woodward DJ-ing in the dark, circa 1980s

Opposite: Jukebox, 1975
Rob Woolmington

a very interesting crew. They were writers and musicians and painters. And I remain friends with them to this day.

All through my life I've associated with Bennington College. It started because I've always been interested in art and being an artist, so I gravitated to the college as a kid. It was like my outlet. Some of my best friends to this day are kids that went to Bennington College, including the guy who bought the diner. I was the one who told him it was for sale. He kept bugging me about it. I let him know when Sonny died and he asked what was happening with the Benn and to let him know. I introduced him to all the staff, I introduced him to the people who were selling the place — I connected all the dots.

It's funny, when people came from out of town, I'd always bring them to the Blue Benn. I wouldn't tell them where I was bringing them, I'd let them find out for themselves. I'd let them discover the kind of place it was. And as we walked through the door, I would have to talk to 12 to 13 people before I got to the booth, and work my way like I'm running for mayor. And they're like, "Jesus, do you know everybody in southern Vermont?" I was like, "Well, yeah."

But that was the Blue Benn. You know what I liken it to? It's almost like an oasis in the desert. You have a watering hole. Now, outside that watering hole, the particular creatures that come down to that thing will probably not get along, but they all come down to that little oasis and all sip from the water, all different walks, from the jaguars and elephants and — as I say, outside of that, they wouldn't maybe get along. But once they come down, they sip from the waters of the Benn, they all sort of get along. And they respect that.

Anthony (TJ) Williams

A Mix Of Regulars

When Anthony Williams was 11 years old, he set off on a trip few people twice his age would hazard. It started with his father, "walking up to the house, with the sunset behind him and fanny pack filled with travelers checks." It wasn't long before he found himself with his two younger siblings aboard a Greyhound bus headed to California. "My parents left it to me to make the decision, and I chose to go." Once in L.A., the three traveled with their father by truck, crossing the border in Arizona and driving some 1,800 miles through Mexico to Belize, the tiny Central American nation parked on the Caribbean Sea. "It was a hell of a trip," he says of the three-month odyssey, musing that the experience taught him resilience, grit and to embrace adventure, even the culinary kind.

I'll be 40 years old in about a week and have lived in Bennington my whole life — I was born and raised here. I have two boys, 13 and 16. I've done all kinds of work over the years, from youth counselor to construction. Right now, I run a construction business and recently was elected to the Southwest Vermont Technical School Board. So you could say I'm a person who keeps evolving.

I don't really remember going into the Blue Benn as

a little kid. My mom had four kids, and when she did go, she'd pack us into one of those small booths, and sit us up in booster seats. But what I do remember is the waitresses. My mom used to be an assistant manager at the Ramada Inn. And a couple of the waitresses — this was when I was very young — worked at the Ramada at that time. Jeannie was one I definitely remember. Actually, I worked with Jeannie years later at the Paradise Restaurant. I was a busboy back then and she was a waitress.

So fast-forward some years and I'm an adult going into Blue Benn — you know, kind of a regular. I used to bring my own kids there from time to time. Sometimes they were picky eaters — you know kids — and you'd get a huge bill and you're like, ugh, they hardly ate anything. So then I started just going there on my own. In some ways it was more enjoyable. You'd go there on a weekend, and the lobby would be filled with people waiting for a booth. But because you're on your own, you go right in, jump on a counter stool and order food right away.

I'm definitely a counter fan. Sometimes it's awkwardly close — you could reach over and grab a tater tot off someone's plate before they even knew what happened [*laughs*] — but you kind of get used to that. I'd get in, get out, and be going about my life while the people in the foyer were still waiting for a booth.

My favorite spot was right in the middle. You had a little more space there to engage in conversation, so you're not like, spitting on each other. [*laughs*]

There's only two meals that I order there. I never even bother picking up a menu anymore. They're what I call bang-for-your-buck meals. So you got a black bean chicken quesadilla, which is huge. It comes with sprouts and vegetables, and I usually get an avocado put in there as well. And there's the Philly cheesesteak omelet with rye bread, dry and uncut, which makes it a hungry-man's sandwich. Eat one of those two meals for breakfast and you know you're not gonna want to eat again till dinnertime. [*laughs*] But they're good. That's it, that's all I ever get there. A creature of habit.

Aside from the food, I think people love the novelty of the environment, or just the fact that it looks as if someone could back up a truck and hook it up and drive it away. I think it's just that oddity of it. It's like this stainless steel railway car got parked here, and next thing you know, there making a fortune here in business. [*laughs*]

Being in the Benn, you did kind of feel like you were stepping back in history or maybe that you're part of history. That's not your goal — you're trying to get a meal and get out and do what you gotta do — but, just sitting at the booth or the counter, being able to put a quarter in the jukebox and press B12 and play Bob Dylan or Patsy Cline or "American Pie" and people start bobbing their heads. It's just a very cool environment.

At left, before and after quesadillas

Anne Mele & Mike Algus

A Mix Of Regulars

To describe Anne Mele and Mike Algus as "foodies" doesn't do the couple justice. For them it's not about sampling the hottest cooking craze on social media or snapping the requisite iPhone pic of a delectable dessert. Mike and Anne crave the adventure of eating, of finding new places to explore and discovering great food along the way. By Anne's count, the couple has visited more than 30 countries, with only two continents — Antarctica and Australia — left to tour. Mike prepares for their trips weeks in advance, sussing out the best places to find mouthwatering local dishes, from top restaurants to local dives. Anne digs a little deeper; "I usually try to take a day course in a local cooking school wherever we go," she says, ticking off Mexico and Sicily as two memorable classes. The longing to jump into a community head first may have been what brought Anne and Mike to Sonny's Blue Benn Diner when they moved to Vermont nearly 30 years ago. "It was so much a part of the community, of the character of the town and you got good food," Mike says. "It didn't take long before we went there all the time."

Mike: We came here 28 years ago. We were living in New Jersey, in the suburbs. Neither of us particularly liked that. It was either move back to the city or try the country. We considered Boston … then a position came up here [at Southwestern Vermont Medical Center] and I always loved Vermont, so we took it.

Anne: We'd been to this area before we had kids and really I liked it a lot. So that was important part of the decision.

Mike: I'm a pulmonary physician.

Anne: And I'm an occupational therapist. We have three kids, daughters, who all grew up here. Our oldest was seven when we moved and then it goes down to the baby.

For us as a family, 2020 was the weirdest year, which I suppose everyone is feeling. …

Mike was the only pulmonologist in Bennington during the pandemic, so that was a lot. And for a hundred days all of our grown-up kids lived with us. Our granddaughter, who was born right before the pandemic, moved in with us with her parents —

Mike: For a hundred days. Yeah, we saw the baby grow up for those three months.

Anne: She was only about three or four months old when she came here. It was great, though, too, because I would never have had that much time with my granddaughter otherwise.

It's funny, when our kids come home usually the first thing they want to do is have breakfast at the Blue Benn. And if they bring friends, that's where they take them. The waitresses always remember them and know who they are, and they love that. This year, well that's obviously all changed.

I think my funniest memory of the Blue Benn is

"It gets back to that thing of everyone knowing each other so well — that sense of community."
— Mike Algus

when I took my daughter Lexi and three of her friends to lunch there when they were about 13. They were at my house and bored and one of them came up with the idea of designing some clothes. So they made these outfits — short skirts, actually. I'm pretty sure they were hand sewn.

They were so proud that they made these things, their designer collection, that they wanted to show off. "Let's go have lunch!" I was like, OK, let's go. And I remember when we got there, one of their skirts started to fall apart at the seams. [*laughs*] It was hilarious. We tried to quickly figure out what to do and I think Sharon or Heidi came over with some safety pins and we all tried to pin it up.

Mike: I missed that scene. [*laughs*]

When the kids were young we'd go every week for dinner — Wednesday and Thursday nights.

Anne: And we'd always see the same people, the Wednesday, Thursday night regulars.

Sometimes, if there were too many of us, some had to sit at the counter and some at the table, because the tables are so small. [*laughs*] When you have a family of five, it's hard.

And then if we were meeting another family, sometimes we would split up; we'd sit at one table, while the kids would sit at another table. And they loved that, so that was fun. It is really a place that gave our kids a lot of memories and a lot of happy times.

Mike: The waitresses were a big part of what made it fun. There were about four or five things I'd ordered pretty regularly, but the majority of the time I'd order a Turkey Mesa.

Anne: Yeah, so they would just make fun of him, that he would never change what he was eating. [*laughs*] He'd say, "Well, maybe I'll have the hamburger." And they're like, "No, you want your Turkey Mesa. Just get it."

Mary Lou was different. She has such a beautiful, gentle spirit. I never saw her angry or cutting.

Mike: Well, she'd get pretty upset with people trying to walk in …

Anne: Oh that, yeah, that's true.

Mike: That was the cardinal rule; you don't just walk in. [*laughs*]

Anne: That's right, don't just walk in here, you tourist. [*laughs*] I always loved watching when new people did it, to see what would happen. Sharon or Heidi or Mary Lou would always be right there with "No, look at the sign! You wait for a booth." Sometimes they were kind of rude about it, too, but it was funny. They even did that with famous people, which I thought was hilarious. [See page 155, Seen at the Diner.]

Eggs Benedict

Mike: That's right. Tourists would come in and they try to walk right in, and we'd all watch them. [*laughs*] It was kinda a game out there in the portico. The corollary rule was never try to sneak your way to a booth from the counter or the waitresses would really yell at you. [*laughs*]

Anne: But really, the waitresses at the Benn were great. We knew all their families, they knew our family, so there'd always be a lot of questions going back and forth. They would tell us what was going on with their kids or other relatives and that was nice. It was nice to go in there — you really knew you were in a small town. They know who you are every time you walk in. That felt really good.

I remember one time, it was close to Christmas, and Sharon presented us with a gift that she had made. She knew that Mike liked to play tennis, so she had found this old tennis racket, and she put a mirror in it. She gave it to us for Christmas. It was so — I mean it was totally unexpected, and so thoughtful.

Mike: And there was the time I left my keys. I'd often — well, everybody would often leave their keys on the table. This particular night I didn't really realize it until we got home. I thought, OK, I'll just pick them up after work tomorrow. So the next day I'm walking from my office to the hospital, and I see Heidi in her car. She's yelling, "Dr. Algus! Dr. Algus! I've got your keys!" So she'd come up to the hospital to bring my keys back to me. It was nice.

Anne: We'd see Heidi a lot in the evening, and Sharon too. Sharon knew that we really liked music, and so she would come and just sometimes sit at the table and start talking about music that she heard, and what have we heard, and do we know about any concerts coming up, and then she would tell us about concerts she knew about. She'd talk to us about things that I don't think she talked to everybody who was there about. She just made us feel comfortable.

Mike: It gets back to that thing of everyone knowing each other so well — that sense of community.

Anne: There's something about going to a place where people know who you are when you walk in, and know your whole history; you can have a nice conversation with them. I miss it. There isn't any place else that I can think of in town that's like that. I think that's probably why we kept going there. It felt comfortable and it felt comforting.

Julius Rosenwald aboard Amtrak's Empire Service, circa 1980s

Julius Rosenwald

A Mix Of Regulars

Misfits is how Julian Rosenwald describes the Williams College class of 1969, relishing his place among the rebels. "Williams was traditional at a time when students were non-traditional, rebelling and experimenting," he says, attempting to describe a time when the Vietnam War consumed the nightly news and student protests rattled the nation. "Looking back at college, the metaphor that comes to mind is an unraveling sweater that the powers that be were desperately trying to knit back together." After graduation, Julius moved a short 10 miles up the road to Vermont. "There were dairy farms, loggers, carpenters and plumbers doing work that made sense to me. People didn't get on a train in the morning, go to an office, and come back at the end of the day, asking themselves what the hell have I accomplished today?" he says. And so he stayed, living in the same Pownal house for 51 years. Settled, but still a rebel at heart.

I was born and raised in Philadelphia. I came to the area in 1965, to go to Williams, so that would be — 56 years, in the general area.

Did you stay in the area because of Williams?

Oh my god, no. When I was applying to college — I'd gone to a wonderful school in Philadelphia, a Quaker school called Germantown Friends School. I had an English teacher, who had been a professor at Reed. He was a great teacher and thought I'd like Reed. When I told my mother I was going to apply there and that it was in Portland, Oregon, she said, "forget it." That was a shame, because I would've probably fit in much better at a less conventional school. I was never particularly conventional.

You graduated from college and were living in rural Vermont. How did you make a living?

I taught school. It was a deferment from the war in Vietnam. I got my teaching certificate in North Bennington, and worked as part of a joint project between Prospect School and the public school system. That qualified me to get a job teaching, and I got a job in Woodford.

I taught there for a total of three years. There were 50 kids in the school and two teachers — a two-room schoolhouse. Then I went to Buxton School in Williamstown and taught older kids, grades nine through twelve. I was there for four or five years.

So you were a teacher, presumably, the rest of your career?

No! No, I'd always been fascinated by the restaurant business, so I worked in a restaurant in Williamstown, and then got into freelance writing. And that's what I did for a long time. Mainly *The Berkshire Eagle* and *The Williamstown Advocate.*

Did you remember the Blue Benn in the early 1970s, before Sonny and Mary Lou owned it?

I do. I first met Sonny — I could've even been in college — right at the Four Corners in Bennington, at the Vermonter restaurant. And he was the night cook. I would stop there for something to eat on my way home at 11, 12 o'clock at night. He would come out of the kitchen to talk or bring your food out. Right from the very beginning — he must've been quite a young man at that point, not much older than me —he was one of those people, just like he was at the Blue Benn, who loved to come out and visit with the customers.

I don't remember the first time I went to the Blue Benn after Sonny bought it, but it pretty quickly evolved into a cornerstone of my life in the area. Before Sonny owned the place, the food was indistinguishable from any other diner. It was nothing particularly unusual.

From the start, Sonny was very prescient about what would appeal to his customers. He was way ahead of his time and an early adopter of health food. At some point early on, he latched onto *The Moosewood Cookbook*. I think that started the Blue Benn revolution, in terms of edibles. He loved experimenting and I think the *Moosewood* was his launch pad.

"Sonny was always concerned about his health. His decision to ban smoking — talk about ahead of his time — was five years ahead of Vermont state law."

— Julius Rosenwald

Sonny was always concerned about his health. His decision to ban smoking — talk about ahead of his time — was five years ahead of Vermont state law. It was a big deal that shook up the local diner world. He knew he was gonna lose customers, but I'd say 95 percent of them came back.

He was interested in the fact that I loved bicycles. Back then I had an English bicycle from a company called Dawes. I was getting rid of it to buy another bicycle, so I sold it to Sonny. The idea of riding a bicycle for transportation and for exercise appealed to him, but I don't think his schedule really permitted it.

Mary Lou was very protective of her time alone with Sonny. I was always fascinated by her. She had the capacity to turn — she'll probably shoot me for this — a very calm situation into something frenetic. If there were two people at one end of the diner, and it wasn't at all crowded, she would still run an order in and rush down the counter to deliver it in a big hurry. She was always going at high speed. As soon as she walked into the diner, she had her foot on the accelerator, pedal to the metal. Meantime, Sonny would be schmoozing with customers, totally laid back. He was just a very sweet guy.

Someone once told me that the highest-paying non-professional job in Bennington was a waitress at the Blue Benn. In other words, unless you were a college graduate with a degree and you were a paralegal or a nurse or something like that, you couldn't possibly make as much money anywhere else in Bennington. That's naturally going to lead to some arguments. The sassy waitress routine was funny and fun, but there was some catty stuff between them that was not particularly nice.

But they were great with the regulars and if they found out it was your birthday. … [*laughs*]

I remember once — I don't know if somebody told Sonny it was my birthday, or he just knew it — he comes out of the kitchen with a muffin with one candle stuck in it. [*laughs*] That, I distinctly remember, and everyone in the place singing Happy Birthday. I probably sent it back and asked him to grill it. [*laughs*]

I loved their grilled muffins. I'd put in the same order for a grilled corn muffin for years, I probably should say, decades, and I couldn't bring myself not to say, "well done." I mean, they knew I wanted a muffin well done on the grill, as if I had it tattooed on my forehead: "well done on the grill." But I couldn't stop saying it.

My Blue Benn favorites? I think probably the most

regular order I would put in was for breakfast — eggs, home fries, and toast, and coffee. I was also a huge fan of his turkey Reuben. Another favorite was always grilled cheese and tomato.

There were three items on the menu that Sonny insisted be made from scratch, and the tradition carried on till the place closed: one was turkey. They roasted a turkey every day. Another was corned beef hash. Corned beef hash from scratch is a really time-consuming process, because I think it takes like six hours to make the corned beef. And the third, which is pretty uncommon, were the French fries which were cut from potatoes with a French-fry maker — you put the raw potato in and it pushes through a grate.

In a lot of ways Sonny felt like he was from a different era. There was a gentility and a formality about him, and a keen interest in his customers that just sort of felt old-fashioned. Sonny was a real gentleman. Polite, courteous, and he took a real interest in people who came in all the time. He was like a barber that way, one of those old-fashioned barbers that really knew the community.

He was also funny. I remember they had what he called the Wall of Shame, behind the cash register. It would happen few times over the years, that you'd order, I don't know, an omelet and coffee, and the bill would be eleven dollars and you'd just have five in your pocket. So they would put your check and your name on the wall behind the register — "Deadbeat Rosenwald hasn't paid his goddamn bill." And it would stay there until you came back and paid it.

It says something about the place that remarkably few people ever cheated them. I bet there weren't a half-a-dozen people who did that. Sonny insisted on a cash-only policy so people, especially tourists, would have to run off to an ATM to pay. I once asked Sonny, "How many times have you been stiffed?" He said it was a minuscule number of times.

It was like that with the waiting room too — an honor system everyone in town understood.

You would be sitting out in the foyer, waiting for a booth, and people — again, you knew they were from the city — they'd walk in and look around and say, "Where do you get your number?" They could not believe that you didn't need a goddamn number to know who was the next person in line. You walk in, and there are four people sitting there: they're ahead of you. Simple.

When you talk about the Blue Benn, the phrase that comes to mind is "community center." It was a true community center. You were always recognized and welcomed there, not because of anything other than that you were a regular. The diner was a gathering spot for everything from the local bank president to the local plumber to people passing through, and so it was truly a gathering place for, and welcoming to everybody. All that, and not at all pretentious.

Somebody at the Chamber of Commerce said the Blue Benn was the second- or third-most visited site in Bennington, behind the monument, Robert Frost's grave — I think the top four were the monument, Robert Frost's grave, Bennington Potters, and the Blue Benn. But certainly it was the most notable restaurant. There was always something comforting about the Blue Benn, a feeling of security that a lot of people counted on, whether they recognized it or not.

Julius Rosenwald, 2021

The Blue Benn

The Benn, circa 1985

John S. Dykes for Yankee Magazine, May 2001

CHAPTER SIX

SPECIALS

SEEN AT THE DINER

As much as Sonny's Blue Benn was a haven for locals, college students and eccentrics of all kinds, it was also a hotspot for celebrity sightings. Hollywood A-listers discovered the diner in dribs and drabs, first arriving in the 1990s when news of Sonny's cooking started to spread.

Most didn't have far to come. Every year, Bennington College and, even more so, the Williamstown Theatre Festival draw an impressive number of famous actors. Far from the long lenses of Hollywood paparazzi, and comfortable in a state that cares little about celebrity — Vermont has a long history of shielding luminaries — the rich and famous ate at the diner with surprising regularity and little fanfare. Staff and regulars took it all in their stride. What follows are a few recollections of the glamorous and the glitzy.

Marisa Tomei / I was sitting in the foyer, waiting for a booth. Marisa Tomei walked straight in, no idea of waiting. And the waitresses were like, "Nope, you gotta go back out there and wait in line like everyone else." She was very sweet about it, and she was funny. She just stayed out in the foyer and talked with everybody. No, it wasn't like the story about Gwyneth Paltrow. [*laughs*] — Anne Mele

Gwyneth Paltrow / Bennington legend holds that when Gwyneth Paltrow and Winona Ryder were still besties back in the 1990s, the two showed up at the diner together. They waltzed through the foyer and headed for a booth. The waitress told them to go back out to the vestibule and wait, to which Paltrow allegedly replied, "Do you know who we are?" The waitress snapped back, "Yes, I do. Now go back out to the waiting room." A response repeated and cheered by Benningtonians for decades, regardless of exactly how the scene may have unfolded.

Heidi Tilley's version:

Yeah. That is a true story. I don't know if it was me or not. I might have done it the first time she came in, because she was in there a few times. She came a lot, with her mother [**Blythe Danner**] and with **Ben Affleck**. He was her boy toy back then.

And Brenda Eggsware's:

I was there that day. People were coming in and saying did you know that Gwyneth Paltrow is out there waiting to come in? When it was her turn, she came in and sat down. I never heard that she [skipped the line]. She used to come in a lot, all the time. Her favorite food back then was fried turkey sausage. Can you imagine?!

And Zoë Sperber's:

About that notorious Gwyneth Paltrow story,

2-Aug-99

For Sonny—
With thanks for the greatest food in the free world!
Lots of love,

Sonny's
Blue Benn Diner

You are about to experience a treat as uncommon as the institution you are now in... the great American diner. Look around you. You are surrounded by history. The ***Blue Benn Diner*** is a Silk City creation, prefabricated in New Jersey in the 1940's. Note the frequency of stainless steel, the barrelled ceiling, the proximity of the kitchen and the fabulous design of the railroad dining car. If the motif intrigues you, wait 'til you try the food! History is now! The choices offered on this menu are fresh cooked, piping hot and suits the aura of a fast vanishing time when good food and fair prices put America on the road.

DAILY
Breakfast and Luncheon
SPECIALS

Your Hosts: Sonny and Marylou Monroe & Lisa Monroe LaFlamme
U.S. Route 7 north, Bennington, Vermont
802-442-5140
Open 7 Days A Week

Inset: 2-Aug-99 For Sonny, With thanks for the greatest food in the free world! Lots of love, Gwyneth Paltrow / Looking toward the entryway, the downfall of more than one celebrity.

who knows if it's true or not. But even if it isn't true, it's people's reaction to it that speaks volumes about Bennington. Everyone loved that story. Everyone was like, "Yeah, you tell 'em! At the Blue Benn no one is better than anybody else!" People still tell that story to out-of-towners, as if it explains Bennington.

Blythe Danner / Once, when it was really slow, Blythe Danner and I got talkin' about all kinds of stuff. We even talked about dating. I said I hated dating and she said she'd lost her husband a while back ... and had no desire to ever date again. Just normal girl talk.
— Brenda Eggsware

Rob Lowe / The place was packed. There wasn't a seat to be had. And Rob Lowe just breezed in, totally under the radar. Nobody in the entire place recognized him, but my friend Amy grabbed my arm and says, "That's Rob Lowe!" She recognized him from the back of his neck; she's just that kind of person. At that point he looked like a Bennington College kid, with horn-rimmed glasses and a full beard, not his pretty-boy look. He was in a play in Williamstown. I think it was Chekhov, *Three Sisters*.
— Jim Woodward

Dr. Jonathan LaPook / CBS News chief medical correspondent Jon LaPook and his wife, Kate, or girlfriend at the time, were in the diner. It was her birthday and Jon asked me to pick out my favorite dessert in the pie case and whether we could sing her "Happy Birthday." I'm like, "Absolutely." So we got Chocolate-Raspberry Bash Pie and sang her "Happy Birthday." You would've thought that I had given him a million bucks. He still, to this day, talks about that story, how nice I was to him and his wife. He gave me a twenty-dollar tip, and at the time, that was huge. That was like, oh my gosh. ... He's just a really nice, down-to-earth man. He'd come into the diner for years and years after that. The whole family did, including his father-in-law [the producer] **Norman Lear**, who lives up the road in Shaftsbury. — Lisa LaFlamme

Wally Shawn / Everyone recognizes this guy from *The Princess Bride* and *My Dinner with Andre*. I waited on him when there was hardly anybody in the diner. I talked to him like I didn't know who he was to be respectful. I never wanted [celebrities] to think they couldn't come in and be comfortable eating. So I asked him if he was here for a visit and he said, "Actually I'm here to give a talk at Bennington College. My brother is a [composer and] professor there." — Brenda Eggsware

James Gandolfini / I was in the diner by myself one day and at the far end of the counter — who's the fellow who played Tony Soprano? Gandolfini? Anyway, I look at this guy — I don't even think I was watching *The Sopranos* at the time — and I looked at him again, and he smiles. A real Tony Soprano smile, and in a diner. I got a laugh out of that. — Bill Fisk

And a few others who have stopped in at the Blue Benn: Drew Barrymore, Claire Danes, Danny DeVito, Flea of the Red Hot Chili Peppers, Edward Herrmann, Audra McDonald, Christopher Reeve, David Schwimmer, Amanda Seyfried and Kathleen Turner.

TV'S MOST MEMORABLE DINER MOMENT

The final scene of *The Sopranos* when the New Jersey crime boss arguably meets his doom — in a diner, with the jukebox playing Journey's *Don't Stop Believin'*. The scene unfolds as Tony Soprano, played by the late James Gandolfini, is seated in the family's favorite diner, flipping through the selections on the mini-jukebox. The tension builds and never lets up until the last shot, one of the most controversial in TV history, and the screen goes black.

CHAPTER SEVEN

MOVING ON

JOHN GETCHELL

Sailors call them waypoints; places along the journey that guide them to their destination. Mariners, like the rest of us, are often blown off course, run aground by unpredictable storms or poorly charted plans. For John Getchell, the new owner of the Blue Benn, the diner has been a waypoint in his life since he first came here as a student. "Certain places have a touchstone quality — the Blue Benn is a waypoint, not just for me but for a lot people," he says, explaining his decision to sink his life savings into a small-town roadhouse. He sits, half-leaning, on one of the diner's blue-topped counter stools. It's after closing and we have the restaurant to ourselves, just us and Pookie, John's two-year-old Mastiff who's sprawled languidly across his owner's feet. John's latest adventure is the sort where there's no real departure point or destination. He has settled in this waypoint, a safe harbor of a kind, hoping to steer the Blue Benn on a new course, all the while staying true to the original map. The diner, he says, has long been "a source of comfort and continuity. . . . The way I see taking it over is that it's not actually my diner. I'm just the steward." A new captain, piloting a venerable ship.

I first came to the Blue Benn in 1981. I was a prospective student at Bennington College, and I was in town coming to visit. I'd bought a Greyhound bus ticket that entitled me to travel anywhere in the continental U.S. for, I don't know, two hundred bucks. I was coming from Washington, D.C., but that's not really where I'm from. My dad was a Foreign Service officer in the State Department, so D.C. was home base, but not a place I'd call home.

My idea was to use the Greyhound pass to visit the colleges that I'd applied to. My parents weren't exactly the types to take me on college tours. God no. They were not helicopter parents. In fact, the most common thing I heard growing up, was that I seemed "unparented," which I took as a compliment.

I got off the bus — I think it was fall — this was back when Bennington still had a bus station. I looked around and somehow got myself up to the college. It was a Friday, which meant a Friday night party. Friday night parties at the college back in those days were serious affairs. I mean, it was shortly after the movie *Animal House* had come out, and colleges everywhere in the country were trying to live up to that paradigm. I remember going to the party and just getting wrecked. The next morning some students brought me to the Blue Benn to recover. I had a Sir Benn Omelette [chicken, broccoli, mushrooms, cheddar cheese, topped with hollandaise]. It was the best thing I ever ate. But more than that, there was an atmosphere and ambience to the place that was just so welcoming. And there was just sort of a buzz, a hum to the place that was extraordinary.

I picked Bennington over Colorado College and University of Miami at Coral Gables — and even a scholarship to the University of Southern California — primarily because I had such a damn good time when I came to visit … and the gorgeous girls. [*laughs*]

We really did have an extraordinary class — an extraordinary bunch of classes, from our class with [the writers] Donna Tartt and Bret Easton Ellis all the way up to [the actor] Pete Dinklage [class of 1991], who I knew at the very end of my tenure there. We were a bunch of crazy kids and we were allowed to be crazy. We were the kids in sunglasses and black trench coats, sitting around the diner smoking cigarettes and drinking coffee. [*laughs*]

When I wasn't in school, even before college, I worked for catering companies in D.C. I worked under some pretty tough taskmasters, hard-core restaurateurs — Nora Pouillon, Barbara Witt. So I had a background in the hospitality industry. But my favorite thing was always diners. When I came here and had that Sir Benn Omelette and subsequently a Blue Benn pesto omelet, and felt the vibe of the place, it set a benchmark. It set a standard that I've judged all diners against, all over the country, ever since. And even with an extensive culinary background at this point, my favorite restaurants are still diners.

At Bennington, I was a theater major. I've always said that catering is a lot like theater in the sense that you're creating a show out of nothing; that you're turning up at a venue, whether a house or an empty auditorium, and you're setting up a whole event. However it's put together it's very much like putting on a theatrical production, where you start with nothing, roll in with all the equipment, put on the show, and at the end break it all down and take it away.

It's a very different mentality from the day-to-day operation of running a restaurant, a retail operation. In the two months that we've been up and running, one of the things that I find both quixotic and comforting about running the diner is the sheer routine of it: getting up at four in the morning and rolling in with Pookie, Brian [the head cook] is at the back door, and he's already in here playing music, and we invariably try to sneak up on him and surprise him — fortunately, he thinks it's funny. Approaching the diner, even in the depths of winter, from County Street, you can smell the donuts being baked. It's just this remarkable sensation. And it's a routine that becomes almost instantaneously muscle memory.

Then there's a whole routine of getting the place open every day. And the same faces and the people who, at this point, invariably open the diner in the morning — people who have done it for a very long time. So I didn't have to roll in and establish protocols. They already have the protocols.

It's no longer a theater per se. Now it's something else altogether; it's really more about my learning how this diner runs. I'm not trying to learn it overnight, because again, it's not about putting my imprint on anything. My imprint doesn't matter. What matters is that the diner stays the same, with certain relevant, twenty-first-century

Donut
Bill Walsh

Opposite:
John Getchell with Pookie, the Blue Benn mascot

changes, like accepting credit cards and having an online presence. The only place where I've asked the town to give me a pass for my own personal eccentricity is that I've got the "sign of the apocalypse" out there [*pointing to a portable marquee stationed outside the diner*]. I bought it seven years ago. I put it in front of my house in Maine, and I changed the sign every single day for seven years. I call it my analog Twitter [*daily ruminations run the gamut from, "What if soy milk is just regular milk introducing itself in Spanish" to "Writing about music is like dancing about architecture"*].

Until a few years ago, I was in the catering business in D.C. I ran it with my wife. We got divorced, and I got left holding the bag, running the catering company on my own, at which point I said, Screw this. I'm out of here. I was just burned out. So I moved to Maine, where I have a family connection and I shifted gears. I started doing renovations on old houses, and writing, and just sort of biding my time.

My friend Jim Woodward told me, at the beginning of July [2020], that Mary Lou had finally decided to sell, the place was on the market, and that there were already offers pending.

I had just sold my interest in the family property up in Maine, so I had a little bit of a war chest, and I came up here. Through Jim, I found out who the main players were at the front of the house and the back of the house. So I said to them, look, if I can buy the diner would you come back? I got the relevant people to say, "Yes, if you can get the diner back, we'll come back and work with you." And that was it. When I got their handshake commitment, I went to the realtor, said, "Here it is. I think

> **"Eggs and Sausage"**
> **by Tom Waits**
> *Nighthawks at the diner*
> *Of Emma's 49er, there's a rendezvous*
> *Of strangers around the coffee urn tonight*
> *All the gypsy hacks, the insomniacs*
> *Now the paper's been read*
> *Now the waitress said*
> *Eggs and sausage and a side of toast*
> *Coffee and a roll, hash browns over easy*
> *Chile in a bowl with burgers and fries*
> *What kind of pie?*

Opposite: The Blue Benn, 1975
Rob Woolmington

Mary Lou's asking price is perfectly reasonable. I don't want to nickel-and-dime her or ask her to compromise. I'll give her exactly what she's asking for. Here's the down payment. Will you accept it?" And they did.

I threw all my eggs into this basket. The closing was on December 23rd — I bought myself a diner for Christmas. Who gets to say they did that?

I knew the place. I knew its track record. I knew its following — I knew what it meant to the town, most significantly. And I knew what it meant to people from the college and people who are not from here. The Blue Benn is an iconic diner. It's been around forever. Any listing of the top diners in New England, not to mention the country, the Blue Benn always gets mentioned, and for good reason.

Once I bought it, I sat down with my start-up team and we went through every item on the menu and really looked at everything. On the average, we raised everything by a dollar, which we thought was reasonable. Some things we actually brought down. But the whole point was that we had to make sure the price point was reasonable, that ideally, the average person can come here, have a meal, and walk away with a carryout bag and have a second half-meal.

I won't talk about the time before Sonny, because that's sort of in the mists of time. But, for the time that Sonny was running the diner, not only did he give them a classic American diner, but he also was really innovative. He created a menu that was ever expanding, that brought cuisines and flavor palettes to this little hamlet in a valley in Vermont that otherwise a lot of people never would've experienced. And he didn't do it in a pretentious way. He did it in a very, very straightforward way — just, "Try this."

When you're sitting in the diner at a certain hour of the morning, and there's no music playing, and the waitresses are getting a little attitude, and they're all regulars in here, and people are talking back and forth, the conversation goes from one end of the diner to the other, and it's very much a twenty-first-century iteration of Norman Rockwell. It's lovely. There's absolutely no pretense about it. In fact, what's really nice is that it really doesn't matter who's in the diner at that point. There's no top-down leadership and so it's kind of an intellectual free-for-all in a lot of ways, people are decent with each other.

I bought the diner simply because I knew the Blue Benn, and I knew pretty much that it couldn't fail. I knew that if I was going to dedicate myself to something like this and really throw all my eggs in that one basket, this was a no-brainer for me. There were certain things I had to do; for one, get the same staff back, keep things the same.

But then, arriving here, it struck me that Bennington had really suffered economically over the years and that the opioid epidemic had hit the town hard. It dawned on me how much it meant to the town that some guy who went to college here 35 years ago was going to invest over $650,000 in maintaining and resurrecting one of the town's most iconic institutions. This did not occur to me before, nor did it occur to me that people would be grateful. I really want to help this town thrive again. I'm not sure how much I can do — at 58, I don't have a whole hell of a lot of time to make a difference — but I can certainly try.

My main feeling about actually taking over the Blue Benn is not that this is MY diner. I'm just the steward. For the foreseeable future, I'm the custodian of the Blue Benn Diner. And my mission is to keep it the same and to honor Sonny's legacy.

The Blue Benn

The Blue Benn

The Benn in winter, 2021

EPILOGUE

AN END AND A BEGINNING

When Mary Lou finished mopping the diner's blue tile floor it was four-thirty in the morning. She told herself she wanted to leave the railcar scrubbed clean and smelling of Lysol before handing over the keys to the new owner on that December day in 2020. In truth, she needed a solitary moment to say goodbye, a last chance to reflect in a place that had defined her life for nearly 50 years.

She ran her hand along the length of the faded yellow counter, memories cascading back from across the years. In her mind, she saw the waitresses, "her girls," taking orders at the blue-cushioned booths and heard the buzz of easy conversation among the customers. But mostly Mary Lou thought of Sonny. "I could just see him at the grill or pulling something off a shelf, or in the apron room downstairs," she says, her voice catching at the memory.

The winter sky was still dark when she pulled the door shut on Sonny's Blue Benn for the last time, leaving the diner keys on the countertop, a paperweight to the contact list she'd written for the new owner. A white-lace curtain fluttered in the window. In a different mood, she might have seen it as a final wave goodbye, but by then her melancholy had turned to resolve: "At that point I was more relieved than sad. We had been through so much over the two years since Sonny died. It was time to move on."

In March 2020, as Covid-19 cases spiked across Vermont, the governor closed all restaurants to indoor dining throughout the state. Some owners tried offering curbside or delivery service to stay afloat, but at the height of the pandemic around a third of Vermont's restaurants shut down entirely, the Blue Benn among them.

Mary Lou locked her beloved diner on March 17, wondering even then if the temporary closing would ever be reversed. Years of tough times had taken a toll on Mary Lou. Sonny, her husband for nearly 60 years, had died a year earlier on December 30, 2019, following a long illness. When Sonny got sick Mary Lou folded her life down, cutting back time spent at the diner and nursing him at home through the final years of his life.

I was 19 and Sonny was 21 when we got married. You make certain promises, one was that we would never put the other in a nursing home. I vowed I would do everything in my power to take care of him, to the very end. He absolutely would've done the same thing for me.

By that summer Mary Lou had decided to sell the Blue Benn. The changes she'd endured — Sonny's death, the pandemic, shuttering the diner —must have felt like an unforeseen tsunami crashing over her life. And when the huge wave slowly pulled back to reveal what was left behind, a way forward finally took shape.

"For a while, we didn't have an answer to the question everyone was asking: 'what's going to happen to the diner?' says Lisa of that tumultuous time in her family's life. "But it was pretty clear that after

Julie Snow for "The Rock Ribs of Bennington Town," 1977

taking care of my dad for so long, my mom needed to start living again. She needed the diner out of her life."

For Mary Lou, as painful as it was to sell the diner, she knew it was the right choice: "I told Lisa and Bill, if I don't sell it now, I never will. I'll drop dead in there."

Her voice trembling, Mary Lou continues:

Covid was the answer to my prayers. I'm sorry to say that, and I feel terrible about what happened to so many people, especially people who lost loved ones, but for me it was a release.

On December 23, 2020, almost 46 years to the day that Sonny had agreed to take over the Blue Benn, Mary Lou agreed to let it go. In a legal closing conducted via Zoom, she sold her roadside hash house and its associated property to John Getchell for $595,000. Looking back, she muses:

In the beginning, when Sonny and I started up, a lot of the real old-timers who came into the Blue Benn, truckers and the like, were used to the way things were and they liked it that way. I'm sure they probably said, "Ah, these two kids ain't gonna make it." We proved them wrong.

Now it's John's turn. I think the community will give him a chance, like they did for us, and I wish him well.

By chance, John too was aching for a new challenge. A Bennington College graduate, his heart had long belonged to the town and to the diner he first encountered as a high school student visiting the college. So when John heard from an old friend in Bennington that the diner was for sale, he jumped at the chance.

I was living in Maine, ready to get out of the renovations business. Construction is a body breaker and I was burnt out. I had started putting together a project — a food-truck court — and I was pretty far along, but when James Woodward called and told me the Blue Benn was up for sale, I dropped the project like a hot potato. … At 58, how often do people get the chance to thoroughly reinvent themselves?

He moved in the midst of the pandemic with his Neapolitan Mastiff Pookie, an affectionate bear of a dog with a fondness for plunking his huge head in strangers' laps. It has been, John admits, a taxing transition with a tricky remit: shake up his own life while leaving the diner unchanged.

Part of rescuing the Blue Benn Diner was that I simply couldn't put my own imprint on it. … The diner needed to be exactly what it's always been. … The diner only has to be the diner. It doesn't have to be anything else. And no one expects it to be anything else, and that's great.

Before signing off on the sale, Mary Lou and Lisa

cleared out five freezers and two coolers full of prepared provisions, everything from tomato sauce to cinnamon rolls to cupcake icing. "We had the freezer food, a full walk-in refrigerator, pantry staples and canned goods," says Lisa. "It was thousands of dollars' worth of food. Some of it we doled out to family and friends, but most of the food went to Meals on Wheels." A final act of kindness to the Bennington community.

For 11 months, while the Blue Benn stayed shuttered because of Covid, Benningtonians waited and wondered if their much-loved hangout would ever open again. When word of the sale spread, the town worried that change was in the works. But when John stepped in, hiring many of the old staff and vowing to keep it the same, there was a collective sigh of relief.

On a recent Friday morning, six locals sit at the counter, like birds perched on a high wire. They lean in over steaming cups of coffee, elbows on the mottled Formica, worn thin over the years by countless customers. Conversation is muted at 6:00 a.m. and it's still too early for jukebox music, but the diner feels strangely reanimated, as if it was remembering what life was like before the pandemic knocked us all sideways.

Heidi Tilley is on the morning shift. She navigates easily between customers, chatting just long enough with one so as not to slow down an order from another. It's a well-practiced ballet and one she's been perfecting in her 23 years working at the diner. She puts a dollop of raspberry jam on my plate. I haven't asked, but she tells me the homemade corn muffin is best with a hint of berry. Service Blue Benn style. The client to my right is chowing down Eggs Benedict with home fries and toast. At the end of the counter, a Vermont lumberjack right out of central casting, teases one of the regulars who's just claimed his blue vinyl counter stool. "You're built like me, low speed and high drag," he tells him, patting his own ample stomach. That gets a laugh and a headshake from Heidi, who looks up at the door as an older couple makes their way to a booth. She smiles; business is picking up.

In the many interviews conducted for this book, a consensus emerges: Sonny's Blue Benn was a rare gem. But the diner was never an immutable fixture. Sonny and Mary Lou understood that to thrive, the restaurant needed to evolve. With them at the helm there was always just that bit more to digest: new cuisines, vegetarian cooking, a smoking ban well ahead of its time. And customers ate it up. With luck, the new owner will ensure the diner keeps evolving while staying true to what made the Blue Benn a Vermont institution.

The reasons for its fame are legendary: Sonny's eclectic menu; the quality of his cooking; the long-serving, dedicated staff and Mary Lou's warm-hearted, energetic management. But perhaps most important to the diner's legacy was the place itself: a quirky haunt that over decades became a community landmark, where friends and neighbors could meet, catch up and be part of a larger public family. In the Blue Benn people looked at each other a little differently, ignored strict social barriers and let tolerance be their guide. "People were people and we were all there to eat," one regular told me with a laugh. The diner taught Bennington to sit with neighbors and listen. That was its greatest legacy.

ACKNOWLEDGMENTS

This book would not have been possible without Mary Lou Monroe and her daughter, Lisa LaFlamme, whose kindness, generosity and encouragement allowed the Blue Benn story to be told.

The Story Project would also like to thank the Blue Benn staff and regulars who generously took the time to talk to us, enthusiastically sharing stories of life at the diner, as well as photos and illustrations. John Getchell, the Blue Benn's new owner, was especially helpful.

We're particularly grateful to Kate Lee Butler for her sage editorial advice, Roheela Malik, our marketing director, for keeping us on track, Leslie Noyes for her astute design suggestions, Suzanne Salinetti of The Studley Press for her kind expertise, Heather Wang for her rapid transcriptions and Tom Fenton and Mary Heffron for their conscientious copyediting.

Finally, we would like to thank Londa Weisman, who imagined the book in the first place and provided steadfast support throughout the project.

SELECTED BIBLIOGRAPHY

Baeder, John. *Diners.* Harry Abrams, 1978

Bovino, Erik. *Breakfast in Silk City: Sonny's Blue Benn Diner and the Dichotomy of the "Diner Experience."* Anthropology & Sociology 205, Williams College, 2017

Ehrenreich, Barbara. *Nickel and Dimed: On (Not) Getting By in America.* Henry Holt, 2001

Garbin, Randy. *Diners of New England.* Stackpole Books, 2005

Getchell, John. *Sign of the Apocalypse: Ruminations and Wit from an American Roadside Prophet.* Skyhorse Publishing, 2017

Gutman, Richard J. S. *American Diner: Then and Now.* Johns Hopkins University Press, 2000

Huguet, Marie-Pierre. *The Blue Benn Diner: A Taste of Americana.* Qualitative Research, State University of New York at Albany, 2001

Hurley, Andrew. *Diners, Bowling Alleys and Trailer Parks: Chasing the American Dream in Postwar Consumer Culture.* Basic Books, 2001

Kaplan, Donald, and Alan Bellink. *Classic Diners of the Northeast.* Faber and Faber, 1980

McCormick, Erin K. *Classic Diners of Vermont.* American Palate, 2018

Oldenburg, Ray. *The Great Good Place: Cafés, Coffee Shops, Bookstores, Bars, Hair Salons and Other Hangouts at the Heart of a Community.* Da Capo Press, 1999

Troyen, Carol, et al. *Edward Hopper.* Museum of Fine Arts Publications, 2007

Terkel, Studs. *Working: People Talk About What They Do All Day and How They Feel About What They Do.* Avon Books, 1974

PHOTO CREDITS

Courtesy of Lisa LaFlamme: Pages 12, 14, 24, 29, 31, 32, 120, 148

Courtesy of Mary Lou Monroe: Pages *x*, 2, 3, 4, 5, 17, 25, 34-35, 46, 47, 48, 52, 59, 60, 63, 69, 79, 100, 110, 114, 122, 130, 144, 150-151, 154, 169

Peter Crabtree: Pages *iv*, 9, 11, 15, 16, 18, 20, 22, 23, 26, 30, 33, 36, 38, 39, 40, 42, 44, 45, 49, 50, 53, 58, 61, 62, 64, 66, 67, 68, 70, 71, 75, 77, 78, 82-83, 85, 86, 92, 93, 94, 97, 98, 101, 102, 103, 105, 108, 111, 113, 115, 116, 117, 118, 119, 125, 126, 127, 129, 131, 132, 124, 135, 136, 138, 140, 141, 142, 145, 146, 149, 152, 156, 159, 162-163, 164, 167

Caitlin Randall and Peter Crabtree are the founders of The Story Project, which creates books of all kinds for individuals, families and institutions. To learn more, please visit thestoryproject.net or write info@thestoryproject.net